SANSA

UNESCO WORLD HERITAGE TEMPLES OF KOREA

SANSA

Association of Korean Buddhist Orders

Bulkwang Publishing

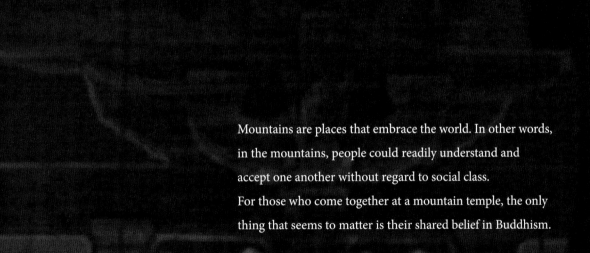

Mountains are places that embrace the world. In other words, in the mountains, people could readily understand and accept one another without regard to social class.
For those who come together at a mountain temple, the only thing that seems to matter is their shared belief in Buddhism.

산은 속세를 끌어안는 장소입니다.
신분의 구분 없이 모두를 그저 있는 그대로
끌어안기에 가장 좋은 장소인 것입니다.
그래서 산사를 찾으면 누구를 만나건
그저 다 같은 불자란 시선 외에
다른 생각은 사라져 버리고 맙니다.

Contents
차례

Tongdo-sa Temple in Yangsan City   008
양산 통도사

Buseok-sa Temple in Yeongju City   044
영주 부석사

Bongjeong-sa Temple in Andong City   082
안동 봉정사

Beopju-sa Temple in Boeun County   118
보은 법주사

Magok-sa Temple in Gongju City   154
공주 마곡사

Seonam-sa Temple in Suncheon City   192
순천 선암사

Daeheung-sa Temple in Haenam County   226
해남 대흥사

Time Line   264
연보

Contents   007
차례

Tongdo-sa Temple

in Yangsan City

양산 **통도사**

The Layout of Tongdo-sa Temple
통도사 가람 배치도

1	Seongbo Museum 성보박물관	13	Yaksa-jeon 약사전	25	Haejangbo-gak 해장보각
2	Ilju-mun 일주문	14	Hwaeom-jeon 화엄전	26	Janggyeong-gak 장경각
3	Yukhwa-dang 육화당	15	Buri-mun 불이문	27	Jeonhyang-gak 전향각
4	Geum-dang 금당	16	Hwanghwa-gak 황화각	28	Diamond Ordination Platform (Geumgang Gyedan) 금강계단
5	Cheonwang-mun 천왕문	17	Daegwangmyeong-jeon 대광명전	29	Daeung-jeon 대웅전
6	Beomjong-gak 범종각	18	Yonghwa-jeon 용화전	30	Myeongbu-jeon 명부전
7	Geungnakbo-jeon 극락보전	19	Bongbaltap Pagoda 봉발탑	31	Seolbeop-jeon 설법전
8	Eunghyang-gak 응향각	20	Gwaneum-jeon 관음전	32	Eungjin-jeon 응진전
9	Yeongsan-jeon 영산전	21	Illohyang-gak 일로향각	33	Samseong-gak 삼성각
10	Three-story Stone Pagoda 삼층석탑	22	Gamno-dang 감로당	34	Sannyeong-gak 산령각
11	Manse-ru 만세루	23	Gaesanjo-dang 개산조당		
12	Yeong-gak 영각	24	Sejonbi-gak 세존비각		

A Place Near to Sakyamuni Buddha

석가모니불을 가장 가까이서 뵐 수 있는 곳

The ultimate goal of a Buddhist is to achieve enlightenment, as the Buddha did. It requires a firm resolve to devote oneself to the teachings of Buddha which will lead one along the path of realization. It also requires one's devotion to protect and preserve the monastic community Sangha that propagates and practices Buddha's teachings. These are the 'Three Jewels of Buddhism': the Buddha(the Jewel of Buddha), the Dharma(the Jewel of Buddha's teachings) and the Sangha(the Jewel of Buddhist community). Three Buddhist temples in Korea represent these 'Three Jewels': Tongdo-sa(the Buddha Jewel Monastery), Hein-sa(the Buddha Dharma Jewel Monastery) and Songgwang-sa(the Sangha Jewel Monastery). Tongdo-sa(*sa* means monastery) represents the Buddha as 'the Temple of the Buddha's Treasure' because of the Buddha's *sarira* enshrined within. These *sarira* or relics of Sakyamuni Buddha were handed down from Bodhisattva Manjusri to Master Jajang[01] of the Silla period, who was studying in China at the time. These genuine *sarira* are specifically referred to as '*Jinsinsari*' in Korean.

불자(佛者)가 된다는 것은 불교를 세우신 부처님처럼 되겠다는 목표, 부처님 말씀에 따라 수행하겠다는 의지, 그리고 그 말씀을 행하고 전하는 승단(僧團)을 보호함에 헌신하겠다는 결심에서 시작됩니다.

이를 각각 불(佛)·법(法)·승(僧)이라고 하며 통칭하여 삼보(三寶)라 합니다.

우리나라에는 삼보를 각각 대표하는 사찰이 있는데 통도사, 해인사, 송광사를 꼽습니다. 통도사가 '부처님'을 상징하는 '불보(佛寶)사찰'인 이유는 신라시대의 자장(慈藏) 스님[01]께서 중국에서 유학하시는 동안 문수보살로부터 직접 전해 받은 석가모니불의 사리를 봉안한 곳이기 때문입니다. 이러한 사리를 특별히 '진신사리'라고 합니다.

●01   590-658.

014

Origin of Buddha's Sacred Relics

Every pagoda in a Buddhist temple enshrines *sarira* believed to be from the Buddha himself, but in actuality, most of their origins are unknown.
The most historically credible *sarira* of Sakyamuni Buddha come from India. There were eight stupas built to enshrine the Buddha's *sarira* following his Mahaparinirvana. Legend says that King Asoka[02] of the Maurya Dynasty, who unified India, enshrined the *sarira* in 84,000 separately erected stupas 100 years after the establishment of the first 8 stupas. If that is true, it may be surmised that every stupa in India holds sacred relics of the Buddha. As such, any *sarira* brought to China and Korea from India was assumed to be those of Sakyamuni Buddha. Some of these relics were brought by Indian monks, or they were obtained by Chinese and Korean monks visiting India. Some *sarira* were also found in pagodas in China, said to have been erected by unknown Indian monks long ago.

[02] He was the first emperor to rule almost all of the Indian subcontinent and a devout Buddhist.
인도 첫 통일 제국의 건국자이자 불교의 열렬한 신자.

부처님의 사리는 어디에서 온 것인가

사찰마다 자리한 탑 안에는 부처님 사리로 여겨지는 사리가 봉안되어 있습니다.
그런데 대부분의 경우 그 출처가 어디인지 자세히 알려지지 않았습니다.
역사적으로 가장 신뢰성이 있는 진신사리는 인도에서 직접 가져온 사리였습니다.
석가모니께서 열반에 드신 후 처음에는 8개의 탑이 세워졌지만, 이후 100년이 지나 인도를 통일한 마우리아 왕조의 아쇼카왕[02]이 이들 탑에 모셔진 사리를 8만4천 개의 탑에 나누어 봉안했다고 전합니다. 이 정도 숫자라면 사실상 인도의 모든 탑 안에 석가모니불의 진신사리가 봉안되어 있다는 뜻인 셈입니다. 그래서 인도의 어느 탑에서 꺼내 중국이나 우리나라로 가져온 사리라면 결국 부처님의 진신사리로 간주되었습니다. 인도의 스님들이 가져오는 경우도 있었고, 중국이나 우리나라 승려가 인도로 가서 받아 오는 경우도 있었습니다. 때로는 정확히 누구인지는 모르지만 중국을 방문한 인도 승려가 오래전에 세웠다고 하는 탑 안에서 사리가 발견되는 경우도 있었습니다.

The Revered *Sarira* of Sakyamuni Buddha Enshrined in Korea

Some of Sakyamuni Buddha's *sarira* enshrined in Korea were recognized as genuine in China and were brought to Korea by Korean Buddhist masters, including Masters Jajang and Uisang. In the case of Venerable Uisang, it is said that Vinaya Master Daoxuan of Tang China loaned to Uisang for seven days a molar *sarira* from the Buddha that he obtained from Heavenly King Indra. With the oppression of Buddhism in Tang China, this *sarira* then found its way to Korea where it was preserved by the Goryeo royal family. However, its whereabouts today are unknown.

Master Jajang was given Sakyamuni Buddha's *sarira* by Bodhisattva Manjusri of Mt. Wu Tai[03] in Shanxi Province of China. Upon his return to Korea, Master Jajang divided and officially enshrined these *sarira* at three sites: Tongdo-sa, the Nine-story Wooden Pagoda of Hwangnyong-sa in Gyeongju, and Taehwa-sa in Ulsan. With the destruction of Hwangnyong-sa's wooden pagoda following one of the Mongol invasions,[04] that *sarira* was lost. After Taehwa-sa was plundered during the Japanese invasion of Korea(Imjin war),[05] its *sarira* was stolen but later returned to be re-enshrined. At that time, the *sarira* were again divided and enshrined at different locations. In view of this history, Sakyamuni Buddha's *sarira* at Tongdo-sa is now revered as the most sacred, having never been removed from its original location of enshrinement.

It is said that during the Goryeo Dynasty, envoys from Yuan China traveled to Tongdo-sa to pay homage to the *sarira* enshrined there. Great Monk Jigong[06] from India is also said to have visited the temple on a pilgrimage. Some of Sakyamuni Buddha's *sarira* enshrined in Korea were taken to Japan during the Imjin War and later returned, along with Joseon prisoners of war. This was due to the efforts of Great Master Samyeong who traveled to Japan to negotiate their return. As you can see, the *sarira* enshrined in Korea have quite a tumultuous history. This legend of Sakyamuni Buddha's *sarira*, bestowed to Korea from Manjusri, Bodhisattva of Wisdom, is a fantastical tale, perhaps difficult to believe without having faith, just as the story of Great Monk Uisang's *sarira*. If it is only the matter of legends, there will be no record of it in historical records. Tongdo-sa's Sakyamuni Buddha *sarira* is a well-known sacred relic of Korea, coveted by all from its early history.

우리나라에 봉안된 부처님의 진신사리

중국에서 진신사리로 인정된 사리를 우리나라 고승(高僧)들이 직접 구해온 경우도 있습니다. 그 대표적인 스님이 자장 스님과 의상 스님입니다.

의상 스님의 경우 당(唐)나라 도선(道宣) 율사를 통해 하늘의 제석천으로부터 부처님 어금니 사리를 7일의 기한으로 빌리셨는데, 후에 당나라가 불교를 탄압하면서 이 어금니 사리가 고려에 흘러들어와 왕실에 소장되었다는 이야기가 전합니다. 다만 현재 의상 스님이 구했던 사리의 행방은 알 수 없습니다.

자장 스님은 중국 산서성의 우타이샨(오대산)·03에서 문수보살로부터 직접 석가모니불의 진신사리를 받아오셨습니다. 스님은 진신사리와 함께 돌아와 공식적으로는 통도사와 함께 경주 황룡사의 구층목탑과 울산 태화사에 나누어 봉안하셨습니다. 그러나 황룡사 구층목탑은 몽고 침입·04 때 소실되면서 사리의 행방이 묘연해졌습니다. 태화사 진신사리의 경우 임진왜란·05 당시 왜군에 의해 약탈되었다가 돌아와 여러 곳에 분산·봉안되었습니다. 결국 유일하게 제자리를 지키고 있는 통도사의 진신사리가 가장 신성한 석가모니불의 사리로서 숭상되었습니다.

고려시대에는 원나라의 사절들이 진신사리에 참배하기 위해 남쪽 통도사까지 내려오는 것을 마다하지 않았고, 인도의 고승인 지공 선사·06 역시 다녀가셨다고 합니다. 임진왜란 때는 왜군이 몰려와 일본으로 반출해 간 사건도 있었습니다. 그러나 사명 대사께서 일본에 건너가 담판으로 조선의 포로와 함께 되돌려 받아 온 파란만장한 역사를 지니고 있습니다.

'문수보살께서 전해주신 석가모니불의 진신사리'라는 전설 같은 이야기는 의상 스님의 사리 이야기처럼 믿음이 없으면 받아들이기 어려운 이야기입니다. 그러나 단순히 허망한 전설에 불과했다면 이런 역사적인 사건은 일어날 수 없었을 것입니다. 통도사 진신사리는 이미 일찍부터 모두가 탐내었던 세계문화유산이었던 셈입니다.

• 03   Chinese Buddhist pilgrimage site of Manjusri(Bodhisattva of Wisdom). Sangwon-sa Temple on Mt. Odae-san in Pyeongchang, where Master Jajang enshrined the *sarira*, carries many Korean legends connected to Bodhisattva Majusri.
중국불교 문수보살 성지, 자장 스님께서 진신사리를 모신 상원사는 평창 오대산에 자리하고 있는데, 이곳은 우리나라 문수보살 성지로서 관련된 여러 설화가 전해지고 있다.

• 04   1231-1259. Mongolia invades Goryeo six times.
1231년부터 1259년까지 몽고가 고려를 여섯 차례 침입한 일.

• 05   1592-1598. Imjin Waeran battle ensued from Japan's two invasions of Joseon.
1592년부터 1598년까지 일본이 조선을 두 차례 침입하여 벌어진 싸움.

• 06   ?-1363. Indian monk, who taught the Korean monk Naong in China; known to have stayed at Sungbok-sa Temple during the Goryeo period.
?-1363. 인도 출신 스님. 중국에서 우리나라 승려인 나옹 스님을 가르친 바 있으며, 고려시대 숭복사에 머물기도 하였다.

帝師新羅國師慈藏律師之眞

Tongdo-sa Temple
양산 통도사

Five Great Sanctuaries of Sakyamuni Buddha's *Sarira*

5대 적멸보궁

Precepts Master Jajang also enshrined the *sarira* of Sakyamuni Buddha in four temples where he personally practiced: Sangwon-sa in Pyeongchang County, Beopheung-sa in Yeongwol County, Jeongam-sa in Jeongseon County and Bongjeong-am Hermitage in Inje County. Along with Tongdo-sa, these five are collectively called *Odae Jeokmyeol-Bogung*, 'Five Great Sanctuaries of Sakyamuni Buddha's *Sarira.*' *Jeokmyeol-Bogung* refers to a palatial structure that enshrines Sakyamuni Buddha's *sarira*.

자장 스님께서는 개인적으로 수행하셨던 평창 상원사, 영월 법흥사, 정선 정암사, 인제 봉정암의 4곳에도 부처님의 사리를 봉안하셨습니다. 그래서 통도사를 포함한 이 다섯 곳을 '5대 적멸보궁(寂滅寶宮)'이라고 부릅니다. 적멸보궁이란 진신사리를 모신 전각을 말합니다.

The signboard, "*Jeokmyeol−Bogung*(寂滅寶宮)," that hangs on *Daeung−jeon*, Tongdo−sa
통도사 대웅전의 "적멸보궁" 현판

A Comprehensive Monastic Compound at the Foot of Mt. Yeongchuk-san

The name of Tongdo-sa Temple comes from the phrase "a place in sync with Vulture Peak Mountain in India." Here, Vulture Peak(pronounced "Yeongchuk-san" in Korean, based on the original Sino-Korean characters) refers to one of the peaks of the five mountains surrounding Rajagriha(present Rajgir), the capital of the ancient kingdom of Magadha, where the Buddha taught dharma numerous times. After passing through the temple's *Ilju-mun* Gate(The One Pillar Gate) and *Cheonwang-mun* Gate(The Gate of the Four Heavenly Guardians), one reaches Tongdo-sa Temple, which is composed of three general areas: *Harojeon*, *Jungnojeon*, and *Sangnojeon*. As each area can also be seen as functioning independently, Tongdo-sa Temple can be considered three temples standing side by side. This layout was also found in Baekje era's Mireuk-sa Temple Site(located in present-day Iksan, Jeollabuk-do Province), which dates back to the Three Kingdoms period. The difference is that the three areas of Mireuk-sa Temple feature the same composition, while the three areas of Tongdo-sa Temple each have unique layouts with their own distinct personalities.

This may be the result of merging various Buddhist orders into one during the Joseon period. However, it is also possible that this layout was intentional from the very beginning when Master Jajang first founded Tongdo-sa Temple. The University of Nalanda, a traditional Buddhist Monastic University located near Rajagriha, also features a similar complex layout. As such, the structure of Tongdo-sa Temple was likely connected to several colleges teaching various subjects. As a Buddhist educational institution, Tongdo-sa Temple may have followed the model of Nalanda University.

Standing in front of *Ilju-mun* Gate, the entrance to the temple, one finds two stone pillars that bear the following inscriptions:

A diverse group of people shall live together, but they must always remain in harmony,
Since they wear monk's robes(*kasaya*) and shave their heads, they must follow the Vinaya(monastic disciplines).

These inscriptions share the same philosophy reflected in the UNESCO Constitution, which says, "Ignorance of each other's ways and lives has been a common cause, throughout the history of mankind," of war. For these reasons, "lasting and sincere support of the peoples of the world" must be founded "upon the intellectual and moral solidarity of mankind."

Tongdo-sa Temple in Yangsan
양산 통도사

영축산 아래 자리한 종합 승원

'통도사(通度寺)'라는 이름은
'인도의 영축산과 서로 통하는
곳[通於印度靈鷲山形]'이란 뜻에서
유래되었다고 합니다. 여기에서 영축산은
인도 마가다국의 수도 왕사성을 둘러싼
5개의 산, 즉 오대산 가운데 한 봉우리로서
부처님께서 많은 설법을 하셨던 곳입니다.
통도사는 일주문과 천왕문을 지나
차례로 하로전(下爐殿), 중로전(中爐殿),
상로전(上爐殿)의 세 구역으로 구성되어
있습니다. 이 각각의 구역은 또한
독립적으로 기능할 수 있는 하나의
사찰로 볼 수 있기 때문에 통도사는 세
사찰이 나란히 연이어 있는 구조라고 볼
수 있습니다. 이런 개념은 이미 삼국시대
백제의 미륵사지(현재 전북 익산)에서도
확인된 바 있습니다. 차이점이 있다면
미륵사는 동일한 구성이 세 번 반복되는
반면 통도사는 각각의 성격에 맞는 서로
다른 구성의 사찰 세 개로 구성되어 있다는
점입니다.
이는 조선시대에 와 다양한 종파가 하나로
통폐합되면서 나타난 현상으로 보기도
하지만, 자장 스님께서 처음 통도사를 세울
때부터 의도된 것일 가능성도 있습니다.
이러한 복합적인 구조는 마가다국 왕사성
인근에 위치한 전통 있는 불교대학인
날란다(Nalanda) 대학에서도 보이는 구조로
다양한 과목을 가르치는 단과대학이
여러 개 연결되어 있었던 구조가 아닌가
생각됩니다. 통도사 역시 그러한 승려 교육
기관으로서 날란다 대학을 모델로 했을
가능성이 있습니다.
사찰의 입구에 해당하는 일주문 앞에
섭니다. 여기에 세워진 두 돌기둥에는
다음과 같은 글귀가 새겨져 있습니다.

異姓同居必須和睦
方袍圓頂常要淸規

다양한 사람들이 모여 살지만
반드시 화목할 것이며,
가사 입고 삭발했으니(方袍圓頂)
항상 그 규율을 따를 것이다.

이것은 '인류는 서로의 풍습과 생활에
대한 무지로 너무나 자주 전쟁을 일으켜
왔다. (이에) 인류의 지적·도덕적 연대 위에
평화를 건설하지 않으면 안 된다'는 골자의
유네스코 헌장의 또 다른 표현일 것입니다.

Mt. Yeongchuk-san is seen in the backdrop of Tongdo-sa Temple. Sakyamuni Buddha gave teachings on Vulture Peak Mountain in the Magadha Kingdom, India. This mountain is often referred to as "holy eagle peak" because its shape resembles an eagle. The stone peak behind Tongdo-sa Temple resembles the stone peak on Vulture Peak Mountain, India.

통도사 뒤로 보이는 영축산. 석가모니 부처님이 설법하셨던 인도 마가다국의 영축산은 봉우리가 독수리를 닮아 붙여진 이름인데, 통도사 너머 저 멀리 보이는 바위 봉우리가 인도 영축산 정상의 바위와 닮아 보인다.

Harojeon, Realm of the Buddhas of the Three Worlds

The three areas of Tongdo-sa Temple face south, but the temple is designed for visitors to enter from east to west. The Three-story Stone Pagoda(Treasure No. 1471) located in the middle of *Harojeon*, the area visitors first encounter, is surrounded by *Yeongsan*-jeon(Treasure No. 1826) to the north, *Geungnakbo-jeon* to the east, *Yaksa-jeon* to the west, and *Manse-ru* Pavilion to the south.

At Buddhist temples, Bhaisajyaguru Buddha(Medicine Buddha) of *Dongbang yurigwang*(Pure Land of the East) is often located in the east, and Amitabha Buddha of *Seobang geungnakjeongto*(Western Pure Land of Utmost Bliss) is often located in the west. However, *Harojeon* is unique in that *Yaksa-jeon*(Medicine Buddha Hall) and *Geungnakbo-jeon*(Amitabha Hall), which symbolize these two respective Buddhas, are arranged with these directions reversed. *Yeongsan-jeon* symbolizes Sakyamuni Buddha and commemorates the 'Turnings of the Wheel of Dharma at Vulture Peak.' Also, *Harojeon* is an area dedicated to the Buddhas of the 'Three Worlds,' with Amitabha Buddha and Bhaisajyaguru Buddha placed on either side of Sakyamuni Buddha.

One element of *Harojeon* that is especially loved by many people is the mural of *Banyayongseon*(the Dragon Boat of Wisdom)

on the back wall of *Geungnakbo-jeon* Hall. *Banyayongseon* is a boat that transports the souls of the dead to the heavenly realm and beautifully conveys the ideal of Mahayana Buddhism. Mahayana means "Greater Vehicle," but also refers to *seowon*(a great aspiration or vow) to become a Buddha and guide all sentient beings to enlightenment. As in the mural, *Banyayongseon*, which transports many souls, is considered as a 'Great Vehicle(Buddhist term Mahayana).' The Bodhisattvas who guide this boat are Avalokitesvara, who is standing at the ship's bow, and Ksitigarbha is at the stern of the ship. They are both eminent Bodhisattvas of Mahayana Buddhism.

Yeongsan-jeon, which was built in 1714, is a hall that symbolizes the Sakyamuni Buddha's 'Second Turning of the Wheel of Dharma at Vulture Peak.' Vulture Peak is especially famous for being the place where the *Lotus Sutra*(Saddharma Pundarika Sutra) was first taught. Among the various *Yeongsan-jeon* murals, the *Yeongsan-jeon* murals of Tongdo-sa Temple in Yangsan(Treasure No. 1711) depict the '*Stupa Samdarsana Parivartah*(Emergence of the Treasure Tower)' from the *Lotus Sutra*. These murals show that the entire hall is a huge illustration of the *Lotus Sutra*.

The vicinity of *Harojeon*, Tongdo-sa Temple. *Yeongsan-jeon* Hall is located in front of the Three-story Stone Pagoda. *Yaksa-jeon* Hall and *Geungnakbo-jeon* Hall are arranged on the left and right of the pagoda respectively.
통도사의 하로전 영역. 통도사 삼층석탑을 중심으로 정면에 영산전이 보이고, 그 좌우로 각각 약사전과 극락보전이 배치되어 있다.

The Mural of *Banyayongseon* on the back wall of *Geungnakbo-jeon* Hall. Sentient beings heading toward the Sukhavati, or Western Pure Land, appear as happy as if going on a picnic.
극락보전 뒷벽에 그려진 반야용선도. 극락으로 향하는 중생들이 소풍 가는 사람들처럼 행복해 보인다.

The *Yeongsan-jeon* Murals of Tongdo-sa Temple in Yangsan
양산 통도사 영산전 벽화

삼세불의 공간, 하로전

통도사의 세 원은 남쪽을 향하고 있지만 동쪽에서 서쪽으로 진입하게 되어 있습니다. 가장 처음 만나게 되는 하로전 영역은 가운데 놓인 통도사 삼층석탑(보물 제1471호)을 중심으로 북쪽에 영산전(보물 제1826호), 동쪽에 극락보전, 서쪽에 약사전, 남쪽에 만세루가 네모나게 둘러서 있습니다.

사찰에서는 보통 동쪽에 동방유리광(東方瑠璃光)세계의 약사불이, 서쪽에 서방극락정토(西方極樂淨土)의 아미타불이 위치합니다. 그런데 하로전은 각 부처님을 상징하는 전각인 극락보전과 약사전이 반대로 배치되어 있다는 게 특이합니다. 한편 영산전은 영축산에서 이루어진 석가모니불의 설법을 기념하는 공간으로서 석가모니불을 상징합니다. 결국 하로전은 석가모니불을 중심으로 좌우에 아미타불과 약사불을 배치한 삼세불(三世佛)의 공간인 셈입니다.

하로전에서 특히 많은 이들의 사랑을 받는 것은 극락보전 뒷벽에 그려진 반야용선(般若龍船) 벽화입니다. 반야용선은 죽은 이들의 영혼을 극락세계로 태워가는 배로서 대승불교의 이념을 아름답게 보여주고 있습니다. "대승(大乘)"이란 '큰 수레(탈것)'를 의미하는데 자신뿐만

아니라 많은 중생들을 깨달음의 세계로 인도하겠다는 의지이자 서원(誓願)을 의미합니다. 벽화에서처럼 많은 영혼이 함께 타고 있는 반야용선도 대승에 해당합니다. 이러한 배를 마련한 분은 배 앞에 타고 있는 관음보살(혹은 인로왕보살)과 뒤에 타고 있는 지장보살로서 모두 대승불교의 대표적인 보살입니다.

1714년 세워진 영산전은 석가모니불의 영축산 설법을 상징하는 공간입니다. 영축산은 특히 『법화경』을 설하신 곳으로 유명합니다. 그래서인지 영산전 벽면의 다양한 벽화 중 『법화경』「견보탑품」을 그린 통도사 영산전 벽화(보물 제1711호)는 이 전각이 하나의 거대한 『법화경』 그림책이었음을 알려줍니다.

Palsangdo in *Yeongsan-jeon* Hall of Tongdo-sa Temple
통도사 영산전 팔상도

The Life of the Buddha in Illustrations
그림으로 표현된 부처님의 생애

Inside *Yeongsan-jeon* Hall is a *Palsangdo* painting(Treasure No. 1041) depicting the Eight Great Events in the life of Sakyamuni Buddha. Here, the method of displaying the eight paintings is unique. Normally, there are four pictures displayed on each side of a Buddha statue. However, in this hall, the Buddha statue sits on the east side of *Yeongsan-jeon* while the eight pictures are hung on the front wall inside the building like a huge folding screen. This *Palsangdo*, regarded as a masterpiece among the existing *Palsangdo*, has been added to Tongdo-sa's Seongbo Museum collection for preservation.

영산전 내부에는 석가모니불의 생애를 여덟 장면으로 묘사한 팔상도(보물 제1041호)가 있습니다. 특이한 점은 8폭의 그림을 불상을 중심으로 좌우 4폭씩 거는 일반적인 방식과 달리, 불상을 동쪽 한켠으로 옮기고 대신 건물 정면에 8폭을 나란히 걸어 마치 거대한 병풍을 펼쳐놓은 듯 배치한 점입니다. 현존하는 팔상도 중에서도 수작이라 평가되어 오고 있는 이 팔상도 원본은 현재 통도사성보박물관에 옮겨져 전시되고 있습니다.

Daegwangmyeong-jeon, Tongdo-sa Temple, Yangsan
양산 통도사 대광명전

Jungnojeon, a Place to Seek the Buddha Dharma

In the *Jungnojeon* area of the temple, *Gwaneum-jeon*, *Yonghwa-jeon*, and *Daegwangmyeong-jeon*(Treasure No. 1827) Halls are arranged in a straight line from south to north. *Gwaneum-jeon* enshrines Bodhisattva Avalokitesvara, *Yonghwa-jeon* enshrines Maitreya Buddha, and *Daegwangmyeong-jeon* enshrines a Vairocana Buddha Triad; these depict the Trikaya, or 'threefold body of Buddha'(Dharmakaya, Sambogakaya, and Nirmanakaya). Hence, Tongdo-sa not only enshrines Medicine Buddha and Amitabha Buddha mentioned earlier in *Harojeon*, but also Maitreya Buddha and Vairocana Buddha in *Jungnojeon*. Therefore, Tongdo-sa Temple is akin to a comprehensive monastic university that covers all the important teachings of the Buddha.

The center of *Jungnojeon* is *Bongbaltap* Pagoda(Treasure No. 471) in front of *Yonghwa-jeon*. It symbolizes Buddha's alms bowl. While entering Mahaparinirvana or complete Nirvana, Sakyamuni Buddha entrusted Mahakasyapa(one of Buddha's ten main disciples), to deliver his alms bowl to Maitreya Buddha, who is predicted to be the next Buddha. The devotion of waiting for Maitreya Buddha is expressed by placing this *Bongbaltap* Pagoda, shaped like a stone alms bowl, in front of

Yonghwa-jeon Hall.

The Bodhisattva Avalokitesvara image enshrined in *Gwaneum-jeon* wears a type of scarf that exposes its arms, and the cloth flowing down from the golden crown appears to flutter in the wind. This is generally regarded as an expression of Bodhisattva Avalokitesvara at Naksan-sa Temple in Yangyang County, Gangwon-do Province. Below his knee is a type of armor called *seulgap*. A Bodhisattva Avalokitesvara statue wearing armor is very rare, and it is still uncertain why the Bodhisattva would wear this.

Overall, *Jungnojeon* reflects a scene from the *Gandavyuha*(chapter titled *Entrance into the Dharma Realm*) from the *Flower Ornament Sutra*(*Avatamska Sutra*), in which Sudhana(a young seeker of the truth) travels to visit enlightened masters in quest of the Buddha Dharma or ultimate truth(*gubeop*). Sudhana meets Bodhisattva Avalokitesvara as his 28th teacher and Bodhisattva Maitreya[07] as his 53rd teacher. The enshrinement of Vairocana Buddha, a symbol representing the *Avatamsaka Sutra*, as well as Bodhisattva Avalokitesvara and Maitreya Buddha, is a condensed expression of the tireless search for the Buddha Dharma.

Bongbaltap Pagoda, Tongdo-sa Temple, Yangsan
양산 통도사 봉발탑

구법의 공간, 중로전

중로전에는 남-북으로 관음전, 용화전, 대광명전(보물 제1827호)이 일직선으로 배치되어 있습니다.

관음전은 관음보살, 용화전은 미륵불, 대광명전은 비로자나 삼신불을 모신 전각입니다. 앞서 하로전에서 약사불과 아미타불을 모신 것에 더하여 미륵불과 비로자나불까지 모셨으니 통도사는 그야말로 부처님의 중요한 가르침을 망라한 종합대학인 셈입니다.

중로전의 중심은 용화전 앞의 통도사 봉발탑(보물 제471호)입니다. 이는 부처님의 발우를 상징합니다. 석가모니불께서는 열반에 드시면서 자신의 발우를 나중에 올 미륵불께 전하라고 십대제자 중 한 명인 마하가섭에게 맡겨 두셨는데, 미륵불을 기다리는 마음을 용화전 앞에 이 봉발탑, 즉 석발우를 놓음으로써 표현한 것입니다.

관음전에 모셔진 관음보살은 팔이 노출되도록 일종의 스카프만을 걸치고 있으며, 보관에서 흘러내린 띠가 바람에 펄럭이고 있는 모습을 하고 있습니다. 이런 모습은 우리나라에선 대체로 강원도

양양 낙산사에 머물고 계시다는 관음보살을 표현한 것으로 간주되고 있습니다. 무릎 아래로는 갑옷의 일종인 '슬갑'을 착용하고 있는데, 이런 표현은 매우 드물게 나타나는 것으로 어떠한 이유로 슬갑을 착용하게 되었는지는 아직 밝혀지지 않았습니다.

중로전은 전체적으로 『화엄경』 「입법계품」의 내용, 즉 선재동자가 깨달음을 구하기 위해 여러 선지식을 찾아 떠난 구법(求法) 이야기를 반영하고 있습니다. 선재동자는 28번째로 관음보살을, 53번째로 미륵보살[07]을 만나게 됩니다. 『화엄경』을 상징하는 비로자나불을 중심으로 관음보살, 미륵불을 봉안한 것은 이러한 구법 여행을 압축하여 표현한 것입니다.

Avalokitesvara in *Gwaneum-jeon*, Tongdo-sa Temple
통도사 관음전 관세음보살상

•07   Maitreya is not yet enlightened, and therefore it is referred to as a Bodhisattva here.
미륵불은 아직 깨달음을 얻지 못하였으므로 여기에서는 '보살'로 칭한다.

Sangnojeon, the Heart of Tongdo-sa Temple

The Diamond Ordination Platform(*Geumgang Gyedan*, National Treasure No. 290), a key site at Tongdo-sa Temple, is located on the north side of *Sangnojeon*. In front of the platform is *Jeokmyeol-Bogung*, which has a hip-and-gable roof that intersects in a "T" shape. Particularly unique, this building has four tablets(*pyeonaeks*) facing four directions. Starting with the tablet of the Diamond Ordination Platform(金剛戒壇) toward the south and traveling counterclockwise, the tablets represent "*Daeung-jeon*(大雄殿)," "*Jeokmyeol-Bogung*(寂滅寶宮)," and "*Daebanggwang-jeon*(大方廣殿)." The tablet of the Diamond Ordination Platform in the south and the tablet of *Jeokmyeol-Bogung* in the north indicate that genuine *sarira* or relics of Sakyamuni Buddha are enshrined in the temple. The tablet of *Daeung-jeon* in the east and the

tablet of *Daebanggwang-jeon* in the west respectively show that Sakyamuni Buddha was a great hero when he dwelt on Earth, and that he became a great light of the Dharmakaya(Dharma-body or Truth-body) when he entered Mahaparinirvana. Unlike other halls, *Jeokmyeol-Bogung* does not enshrine any images of Buddha, which is a common feature only among the five *Jeokmyeol-Bogung* in Korea. Instead of an image or statue of Buddha, an open window behind the Buddha altar reveals the Diamond Ordination Platform. People chant prayers inside the hall while facing the platform. It is a visual device that reinforces the fact that the genuine *sarira* of Sakyamuni Buddha enshrined within the Diamond Ordination Platform do not require any substitute statues or paintings. The design of the Diamond Ordination Platform is different from other pagodas

The vicinity of *Sangnojeon*, Tongdo-sa Temple
통도사 상로전 영역

in Korea. Its style is also called *seokjong* because it looks like a stone bell. The design originates from the style of dome-shaped stupas, which are Buddhist structures common in India. Although multi-story, rectangular Buddhist pagodas were popular in East Asia, it seems that architects of the Silla period wanted to honor the genuine *sarira* of Sakyamuni Buddha in the Indian Buddhist style. So, they must have collected information about stupas in India and built this dome-shaped stupa.

Currently, it is prohibited to enter the Diamond Ordination Platform. But, in the past, the *sugye*,[08] ordination rituals were performed on the platform where the stone bell-shaped pagoda is enshrined and one could enter it through one of the four doors located at each of the four directions. That is why the platform is called *gyedan*, meaning a "*dan*"(platform) where monks receive "*gye*"(monastic precepts prescribed by Sakyamuni Buddha) to become ordained. With this *gyedan*, the Buddhist order of the Silla period was finally able to establish a system to ordain monks. Overall, it is reminiscent of Borobudur Temple in Indonesia, and the similarity seems to hide the secret of an extensive Buddhist network existing between these two World Heritage sites.

After touring the *Jeokmyeol-Bogung* and Diamond Ordination Platform, one stands in front of *Myeongbu-jeon*. *Myeongbu* is the netherworld where one is punished for their wrongdoings. Although *Myeongbu-jeon* has a negative connotation, the various folk paintings on the wall make it the most peaceful and beautiful such structure in the world. Perhaps it is so peaceful because it is the closest one to Buddha.

The Diamond Ordination Platform (*Geumgang Gyedan*) at Tongdo-sa Temple
통도사 금강계단

통도사의 핵심 공간, 상로전

상로전에는 통도사의 핵심 공간인
금강계단(국보 제290호)이 북쪽에 있고,
그 앞으로 마치 팔작지붕의 건물이
'정(丁)'자형, 혹은 'T'자형으로 교차해
있는 듯한 적멸보궁이 배치되어 있습니다.
특이한 것은 이 전각에 방향을 달리한 서로
다른 네 개의 편액이 걸려 있다는 점입니다.
남쪽 "금강계단" 편액부터 반시계방향으로
걸린 "대웅전", "적멸보궁", "대방광전"
편액이 그것인데, 남쪽의 "금강계단"과
북쪽 "적멸보궁"은 이곳에 석가모니불의
진신사리가 모셔져 있음을 상징하며,
동쪽의 "대웅전"과 서쪽 "대방광전"은
각각 부처님께서 지상에 머무실 때는 큰
영웅으로, 그리고 열반에 드시면서 법신의
큰 빛이 되셨음을 극적으로 보여줍니다.
다른 전각들과 달리 이 안에는 어떠한
불상도 모셔져 있지 않습니다. 이는 5대
적멸보궁의 공통된 특징으로 불상 대신
불단 뒤편으로 창이 뚫려 있어서 그
너머로 금강계단이 보입니다. 우리들은 그
공간을 통해 법당 안으로 밀려 들어오는
금강계단에 예불을 드립니다. 그만큼
금강계단의 진신사리는 그 어떤 대체물도
필요하지 않은, 석가모니불 그 자체임을
시각적 장치를 통해 각인시키는 것입니다.
금강계단은 우리나라의 일반적인 탑과는

그 생김새가 다릅니다. 마치 돌로 만든
종처럼 생겼다고 해서 "석종(石鐘)"이라고도
부르는데 이러한 모양은 기본적으로 인도의
불탑(佛塔)인 스투파에서 기원한 것입니다.
비록 동아시아에서는 다층의 누각형
불탑이 유행했지만 신라의 건축가들은
석가모니불의 진신사리만큼은 인도의
예법으로 모시고자 했던 것 같습니다.
그래서 그들 나름대로 인도의 스투파에
대한 정보를 모아 이처럼 둥근 형태의
불탑을 만들었을 것입니다.

The folk painting on the wall of *Myeongbu-jeon* Hall
통도사 명부전의 민화풍 그림

현재 금강계단 안으로 들어갈 수 없지만 과거에는 사방의 네 문으로 들어가 석종을 둘러싼 단 위에서 수계(受戒)의식·⁰⁸을 행했다고 합니다. 그래서 '계를 받는 단'이란 의미로 "계단(戒壇)"이라 한 것이니 일종의 학위 수여식장인 셈입니다. 이 계단을 통해 신라의 불교 교단은 비로소 체계를 갖추고 승려들을 배출할 수 있게 되었습니다. 전체적으로는 마치 인도네시아 보로부두르 사원을 연상케 하는데, 이 두 세계문화유산의 유사성 속에 거대한 불교 네트워크의 비밀이 숨겨져 있는 듯합니다.

적멸보궁과 금강계단을 둘러본 뒤 명부전 앞에 섭니다. 명부(冥府)란 지옥으로서 죽은 뒤 생전 저지른 죄에 대한 벌을 받는 곳입니다. 그런 명부를 상징하는 전각임에도 통도사 명부전에는 다양한 민화풍 벽화가 그려져 있어 세상에서 가장 평화롭고 아름다운 명부가 되었습니다. 아마도 부처님 가장 가까이에 있는 명부이기 때문에 그런 것 같습니다.

•08 A Buddhist ordination ritual where one pledges to follow certain principles(rules) as the first gateway to becoming a disciple of Buddha.
부처님의 제자가 되기 위한 첫 관문으로서 지켜야 할 계율(규칙)에 대한 서약을 하는 의식.

Buseok-sa Temple

in Yeongju City

영주

부석사

The Layout of Buseok-sa Temple
부석사 가람 배치도

1 *Jong-gak*
   종각

2 *Beomjong-ru*
   범종루

3 *Bojang-gak*
   보장각

4 *Jijang-jeon*
   지장전

5 *Anyang-ru*
   안양루

6 Stone Lantern
   석등

7 *Samseong-gak*
   삼성각

8 Floating Rock *(Buseok)*
   부석

9 *Muryangsu-jeon*
   무량수전

10 *Seonmyo-gak*
   선묘각

11 Three-story Stone Pagoda
   삼층석탑

12 *Josa-dang*
   조사당

13 *Eungjin-jeon*
   응진전

14 *Jain-dang*
   자인당

Transplanting Bodhgaya of India

보드가야를 옮겨 오다

Buseok-sa Temple in Yeongju City, Gyeongsangbuk-do Province, was founded by Master Uisang,[01] who first established the School of the *Flower Ornament Sutra*(*Avatamska Sutra*)[02] in Silla. Master Uisang built ten temples dedicated to the Flower Ornament School including Buseok-sa Temple. All of these temples were built in northern Gyeongsang-do and Jeolla-do Province, which are areas outside the Silla capital of Gyeongju.

Because the temples he founded were mostly located in areas bordering Silla, some saw these temples, which were constructed in frontier areas, as an attempt to win over Goguryeo and Baekje and to boost the morale of Silla troops. However, Master Uisang's true intention was to find suitable locations for Buddhist practice, and thus, he built temples in remote areas. It is possible that because Buseok-sa Temple was built deep in the mountains, its two Goryeo period buildings remain to this day as some of the last such buildings in Korea.

경북 영주 부석사는 우리나라에 처음 화엄종파[02]를 세운 의상(義湘) 스님[01]이 창건한 절입니다. 의상 스님은 부석사를 포함하여 '화엄십찰'이라고 하는 10곳의 사찰을 세웠는데, 이들은 모두 신라의 수도였던 경주의 외지인 경상도 북부, 전라도 등에 세워졌습니다.

의상 스님이 창건한 사찰들이 대부분 신라 접경 지대에 위치했던 것에 대해서 혹자는 최전방에 이러한 사찰들을 세워 밖으로는 고구려·백제를 포섭하고, 안으로는 신라 장병들의 사기를 고취하기 위한 것이었다고 보는 경우도 있습니다. 하지만 의상 스님은 순수한 의도로 참된 수행을 위해 적합한 장소를 찾아 그러한 외지에 절을 세운 것으로 생각됩니다. 그렇게 깊은 산속에 절을 세운 까닭인지 부석사에는 우리나라에서 몇 채 남지 않은 고려시대 건축물 2채가 남아 있습니다.

01 625~702. A Buddhist master of the Silla Kingdom.
625~702. 신라 시대 승려.

02 *Hwaeom* School, a Buddhist School whose fundamental scripture is the *Avatamsaka* Sutra or *Flower Ornament Sutra*.
『화엄경』을 근본 경전으로 삼는 불교의 종파.

Buseok-sa Temple, Yeongju
영주 부석사

Buseok-sa Temple
영주 부석사

Statue of Master Uisang in *Josa-dang* Hall, Buseok-sa Temple
부석사 조사당 의상대사상

Master Uisang's Studies Abroad

Master Uisang traveled to Tang China in order to study the teachings of the *Flower Ornament Sutra*.

While studying in Tang, he learned about the Flower Ornament School from Great Master Zhiyan at Jisang-sa Temple on Mt. Zhongnan. There, Uisang studied alongside Master Fazang, who succeeded Master Zhiyan to lead the Flower Ornament School in China.

The following is a famous anecdote about Master Uisang and Seonmyo from those times.

It is said that after Master Uisang's boat arrived at Tengzhou in Shandong Province, he found a place to stay, and the daughter of the house owner, Seonmyo, loved him with great devotion. However, being a Buddhist monk, he had to refuse her love and left for Mt. Zhongnan to find his teacher. Yet, as he could not completely reject the hospitality of the host, he promised to stop by on his way back home. However, while staying in Jisang-sa Temple, Master Uisang received information that Tang China would soon attack Silla, and he hurriedly boarded a boat to return home, breaking his promise. But with the fate of his country at stake, he had no other choice. Hearing this, Seonmyo quickly packed a gift for

him and hurried to the harbor, but his boat had already left. Seonmyo, wanting to follow the Master even if it meant her death, threw herself into the sea and turned into a dragon to protect Master Uisang. This story is found in *Song Gaoseng Zhuan*(Biographies of Eminent Monks, compiled during the Song Dynasty).[03] It led to widespread respect for Master Uisang while also becoming widely popular, not only in Korea but also in China and Japan. After informing the royal court about Tang China's intention, Master Uisang immediately went to Naksan-sa Temple in Yangyang and had a personal audience with Bodhisattva Avalokitesvara before heading to Yeongju City. His actions indicate that he intentionally distanced himself from the royal family to whole-heartedly focus on his practice.

의상 스님의 유학 시절

의상 스님은 화엄불교를 배우기 위해 당나라로 유학을 다녀오신 분입니다. 당나라 유학 시절 스님은 종남산 지상사에서 고승 지엄(智儼) 스님으로부터 화엄종을 배웠습니다. 지엄 스님을 계승하여 중국 화엄종을 이끌었던 법장(法藏) 스님과는 동문이었습니다. 스님이 유학할 당시 선묘(善妙)와의 일화는 유명합니다.

배가 산동성 등주에 도착하여 스님이 묵게 된 집의 딸 선묘는 의상 스님을 극진히 사랑했다고 전합니다. 하지만 스님은 출가자의 신분이므로 선묘의 사랑을 마다하고 스승을 찾아 종남산으로 떠나야만 했습니다. 다만 집주인의 호의를 완전히 거절하지는 못해 돌아가는 길에 반드시 들르겠다고 약조했지요. 그런데 지상사에 머무르던 의상 스님은 당나라가 곧 신라를 침공할 것이라는 정보를 얻어 급히 귀국길에 오르는 바람에 약속을 지키지 못하고 배에 오르게 되었다고 합니다. 나라의 운명이 걸린 일이니 어쩔 도리가 없었을 것입니다. 선묘가 이 사실을 알고 신라로 돌아가는 스님에게 드리려던 예물을 챙겨 항구로 서둘러 나왔지만 배는 이미 떠난 다음이었습니다. 이에 죽어서라도 스님을 따라가겠다고 바다에 몸을 던진

선묘는 결국 용이 되어 이후 의상 스님을 지켜주었다고 합니다. 『송고승전』[03]에 실린 이 이야기는 의상 스님에 대한 존경이 널리 퍼지면서 우리나라뿐 아니라 중국과 일본에서도 널리 유행하게 되었습니다. 한편 귀국하자마자 조정에 당의 침공 첩보를 전한 의상 스님은 왕실 근처를 배회하지 않고 곧바로 양양 낙산사로 걸음을 옮겨 관음보살을 친견하셨으며, 이어 영주로 내려갔습니다. 이러한 스님의 행보를 통해 오직 수행 일념으로 왕실과는 일부러 거리를 두려 하셨다는 점을 알 수 있습니다.

- 03 A book containing the biographies of 533 eminent Buddhist monks, written by Master Zanning of Song, China.
중국 송대의 승려인 찬녕의 저술로 고승 533명의 전기를 수록한 책.

The Road to the Western Pure Land of Utmost Bliss

On the way to Buseok-sa Temple, the first thing one notices is an enormous stone embankment, also called "*Daeseokdan*(large stone platform)." It still bears the marks left by wedges driven into the stones by Silla stone masons. One can almost hear the sound of chisels breaking stone. The stairs up the embankment are so steep and high that some people used to say in jest, "If your knees ache, the Western Pure Land is not yours." Such a saying demonstrates how steep and high up the platform goes towards the temple.

At Buseok-sa Temple, the buildings are supported by nine layers of stonework due to the mountain's slope. This is interpreted to symbolize the term "Seven Places, Nine Times" from the *Flower Ornament Sutra*.[04] At first glance, the arrangement of the stones appears random, but actually, they are uneven stones that have been shaped as little as possible and stacked with great care to appear as if they naturally fit together. The advantage of this is that the stonework looks natural while also being solidly interlinked.

Cut through the center of the stone embankment are stairs going from *Cheonwang-mun* Gate up to *Muryangsu-jeon* Hall. At a glance, it appears to be a path from north to south, but in fact, it goes in a southwest direction to *Beomjong-ru* Pavilion(Bell Pavilion), and then turns south after that; its axis curves once. Although this could be interpreted as a result of the path conforming to the topography, it is actually the result of an intentional visual consideration. If the buildings were arranged in a straight line, the buildings in back would be concealed by the buildings in front. However, thanks to the curved path, *Muryangsu-jeon* Hall, the rearmost building, is not blocked from view.

The first building one notices upon entering the compound is *Beomjong-ru* Pavilion. This structure, built around the 18th century, is distinctive for its hip-and-gable roof in front and gable-roof in back. One characteristic of Eastern architecture is that the longest side of a building is the front. This is contrary to Western architecture, where the shorter side is the front. However, *Beomjong-ru* Pavilion at Buseok-sa Temple is unique in that its lateral side, which features the gables of the hip-and-gable roof, faces front, which makes the shorter side of the building the front side when viewed from the entrance. Perhaps, *Beomjong-ru* Pavilion was thought of as a kind of bridge or a dock for ferries. In other words, it conveys the concept of connecting this world and the Pure Land. Moreover, the pillars that support *Beomjong-ru* Pavilion are not entirely smoothed down and retain the natural, curved look of trees. Thus, the shadows of the pillars made by the sunlight in late afternoon, remind one of a primitive forest.

Having passed *Beomjong-ru* Pavilion, one encounters a second building which is *Anyang-ru* Pavilion. Passing through a pavilion on the way to a Dharma Hall is common in Joseon period temples. However, having two pavilions, such as at Buseok-sa, is quite rare. It is presumed that such an arrangement resulted because there used to be another Buddhist structure between *Beomjong-ru* Pavilion and *Anyang-ru* Pavilion.

The term *anyang*(comfort and gratification) refers to the Western Pure Land of Utmost Bliss. That is because the beauty of the scenery here makes one feel they have arrived in the Pure Land. Because the pavilion protrudes forward, it is the optimal place to enjoy the scenery while feeling you are suspended in midair. Originally, pavilions such as this one belonged exclusively to aristocrats and nobles, but eventually they were built at temples too. As a result, commoners were also able to enjoy such pavilions. Pavilions changed from a place enjoyed by only a privileged few to a place for all.

Daeseokdan(large stone platform) at Buseok-sa Temple
부석사 대석단

Beomjong-ru Pavilion at Buseok-sa Temple. On a sunny day, the shadows of the columns harmonize with the natural curves of the trees, giving the impression of entering a primeval forest.
부석사 범종루. 볕이 좋을 때는 누각 기둥이 이루는 그림자를 볼 수 있는데, 구불구불한 기둥들의 그림자가 이루는 조화가 마치 원시림에 들어온 느낌을 준다.

극락에 오르는 길

부석사를 오르는 길에 먼저 눈에 띄는
것은 층층히 단을 지으며 올라가는 거대한
축대입니다. '대석단'으로 불리기도 하는
이 축대에는 그것을 이루는 돌들에 신라
석공들이 채석하기 위하여 사용했던 쐐기
자국이 그대로 남아 있어 마치 정질하던
소리가 들리는 듯합니다. 언젠가 어떤 분이
석단 계단을 오르면서 "무릎이 아프면
극락도 못 가것네."라고 하는 것을 듣고
웃음이 났던 기억이 있습니다. 그만큼 높고
가파릅니다.

부석사는 산의 경사면에 9단의 석축을
쌓아 건물을 세웠는데, 이러한 이유로
『화엄경』의 7처9회'04 설법을 상징하는
것으로 해석되기도 합니다. 언뜻 자연석을
아무렇게나 쌓은 것 같지만 사실 최소한의
손질로 울퉁불퉁한 돌들을 원래 제짝이었던
것처럼 적재적소에 꼭 들어맞게끔
쌓은 것입니다. 이러한 기법은 석축이
자연스러워 보이면서도 더 단단하게
결합되는 장점이 있습니다.

석단 가운데로는 천왕문에서
무량수전으로 오르는 계단이 뚫려
있습니다. 언뜻 남북으로 놓인 길 같지만
범종루까지는 실제 남서향, 범종루를
지나서는 남향이어서 축선이 한 번 꺾여
있습니다. 지형에 순응한 결과로 볼 수도

있지만 이것은 의도된 시각적 배려입니다. 만약 건물들을 일직선으로 배치했다면 앞에 있는 건물에 가려져 뒤에 있는 건물은 보이지 않았을 것입니다. 그러나 지금처럼 축선을 휘어놓은 덕분에 가장 뒤에 있는 무량수전이 가려지는 일 없이 그 존재감을 드러냅니다.

진입하며 가장 먼저 눈에 들어오는 것은 범종루입니다. 18세기 무렵 지어진 이 전각은 앞은 팔작지붕이고 뒤는 맞배지붕인 것이 특징입니다.

동양 건축물의 특징 중 하나는 대개 옆으로 길게 놓인 면이 정면입니다. 짧은 쪽 면이 정면인 서양과는 대조적입니다. 그런데 부석사 범종루는 팔작지붕의 박공이 보이는 측면이 정면을 향하고 있어 진입로상에서 보면 건물의 좁은 쪽이 정면으로 되어 특이합니다. 아마도 범종루를 일종의 다리 혹은 나룻터의 개념으로 생각한 듯 싶습니다. 다시 말해 이승과 극락을 연결해 주는 개념인 셈입니다. 이와 함께 범종루를 받치고 있는 기둥들은 완전히 다듬지 않아 구불구불한 나무 본래의 모습 그대로입니다. 이 때문에 느지막한 오후 햇살에 기둥들이 이루는 그림자는 마치 원시림을 방불케 합니다.

범종루를 지나면 두 번째 누각인 안양루(安養樓)를 만납니다. 누각을 지나 법당으로 나아가는 방식은 조선시대 사찰에서 흔히 볼 수 있지만 부석사처럼 누각이 이중으로 배치된 경우는 흔치 않습니다. 아마도 원래는 범종루와 안양루 사이에 또 하나의 불전 건축물이 있었기 때문에 이러한 구성이 되었던 것 아닌가 추측됩니다.

'안양(安養)'이란 극락정토를 의미합니다. 실제 이곳에서 눈앞에 펼쳐진 풍광을 바라보면 극락정토에 와 있는 듯 아름답습니다. 누각이 앞으로 돌출된 덕에 마치 공중에 떠 바라보는 것처럼 풍광 감상에는 최적화된 공간입니다. 원래 이와 같은 누각은 귀족과 양반의 전유물이었지만 사찰에도 점차 세워져 평민들도 이곳에 올라 풍광을 즐길 수 있게 되었습니다. 특정 계급에만 향유되던 건축물이 모두를 위한 건축물로 변화한 것입니다.

•04 The *Flower Ornament Sutra* contains stories of 9 sermons given in 7 places, therefore the term "Seven Places, Nine Times."
『화엄경』은 7곳의 장소에서 9번 이루어진 설법 내용으로 구성되어 있어 '7처9회'라 표현한다.

Anyang-ru Pavilion at Buseok-sa
부석사 안양루

The hip-and-gable roof and gable roof
팔작지붕과 맞배지붕

"Hip-and-gable roof" and "gable roof" are two terms frequently encountered in descriptions of traditional Korean architecture. The gable roof is the earliest form of roof and it resembles a book placed upside down. On the other hand, the hip-and-gable roof extends out on either side like bird wings to effectively protect the building's side walls. This architectural style is mainly used in key temples and palaces.

우리나라의 옛 건축물에 대한 설명에서 자주 만나게 되는 용어 중 하나가 '팔작지붕'과 '맞배지붕'입니다. 맞배지붕은 마치 펼친 책을 엎어 놓은 것과 같은 형태로 가장 이른 시기에 나타난 지붕 형식입니다. 한편 팔작지붕은 맞배지붕의 양 옆에 지붕을 날개처럼 덧대어 건물의 측면을 효과적으로 보호하기 위한 형식으로 사찰이나 궁궐의 중요한 전각에 주로 사용되었습니다.

The roof of *Beomjong-ru* Pavilion at Buseok-sa Temple is a mixture of hipped-and-gable roof(left) and gable roof(right).
부석사 범종루는 정면은 팔작지붕(원), 후면은 맞배지붕(오)인 독특한 전각이다.

The Charm of *Muryangsu-jeon* Hall

The sanctum in the heart of Buseok-sa Temple is *Muryangsu-jeon* Hall(National Treasure No. 18). At first glance, the unadorned pillars, crossbeams, and purlins of this wooden structure may seem ordinary, but each pillar and crossbeam is a perfect work of art.

The front of Buseok-sa's *Muryangsu-jeon* Hall, which stretches from left to right, measures five *kans*[05] across. Such a building might seem boring and repetitive, but a careful look reveals that each of the five *kan* differs in width. The central *kan* is the widest, and the *kan*s on either side become progressively narrower, with the end *kan*s being narrowest. The progressive narrowing of each *kan* is a basic technique of classical Korean architecture, and therefore, cannot be said to be unique to *Muryangsu-jeon* Hall. Yet, the rate at which each *kan* narrows is determined by the architect, giving each structure its own character.

Buseok-sa's *Muryangsu-jeon* Hall gives the impression that the middle *kan* is pushing outward to the left and right, appearing to squeeze out the *kan*s on both sides. In other words, the structure conveys a sense of motion, making it appear as if it is growing from the inside out.

Meanwhile, the eaves lift slightly upward, like a flying crane. While the lines of the eaves in Korean traditional architecture are generally quite beautiful, such delicate yet powerful curved lines appear both solemn and cheerful at the same time. Thus, the horizontal sense of movement stretching left and right at *Muryangsu-jeon* Hall is simultaneously combined with a vertical sense of movement that makes one feel as if the building is flying.

●05 A unit of measurement referring to the distance between two columns.

Muryangsu-jeon at Buseok-sa Temple, Yeongju
영주 부석사 무량수전

무량수전의 매력

부석사의 중심 불전은 무량수전(국보 제18호)입니다. 언뜻 아무런 장식 없이 오로지 기둥과 대들보, 도리가 얽힌 평범한 목조 건축물로 보일지 모릅니다. 하지만 전각의 대들보와 기둥은 그 자체로 완벽한 장식이 됩니다.

부석사 무량수전은 좌우로 긴 전각으로서 정면이 5칸입니다. 이런 건축물은 기차처럼 반복적인 느낌이 들 수 있어 자칫 지루해 보일 수 있습니다. 하지만 자세히 보면 5칸의 간격이 조금씩 다릅니다. 가운데 칸이 제일 넓고 좌우로 갈수록 좁아져서 맨 끝 칸의 간격이 가장 좁습니다. 이렇게 갈수록 칸을 줄이는 것은 고전건축 기법의 기본이기 때문에 무량수전만의 매력이라고 할 순 없습니다. 다만 건축가의 감각에 따라 줄어드는 정도가 달라짐으로써 매력 또한 달라집니다.

부석사 무량수전은 마치 가운데 칸이 좌우로 팽창하면서 옆 칸으로 갈수록 압력을 받아 좁아진 듯한 느낌이 듭니다. 다시 말해 안에서 바깥으로 뻗어 나가는 운동감이 느껴진다는 게 중요한 포인트입니다.

한편 지붕의 처마는 마치 한 마리 학이 나는 것처럼 가뿐하게 치켜 올라가 있습니다. 우리 옛 건축물의 처마선은 대체로 아름답지만 이처럼 은은하면서도 강렬한 곡선은 유독 장중하면서도 경쾌한 느낌이 들게 합니다. 그래서 무량수전에서는 좌우로 펼쳐지는 횡적인 운동감과 날아갈 듯한 수직적 운동감이 동시에 느껴지지요.

The Highlight of *Muryangsu-jeon* Hall: Entasis Columns

Moreover, looking at the slender columns – neither too thick nor too thin – in contrast to the building's magnificent structure and complex bracket system[06] on the pillars, reminds one of a flower. It looks like a flower is supporting the roof, and it makes the roof appear weightless. The central part of the columns bulge outward, a style known as "entasis." But why were the pillars shaped this way? If you consider only their visual appearance, they seem to swell in the middle due to the weight pushing down from above. If they were normal columns, the force applied by the roof would appear to be stopped by the pillar, however, in the curved column, the pressure does not dissipate. Moreover, having swelled up so tight, the force appears as if it could bounce back at any moment. The architects of *Muryangsu-jeon* Hall intended to make it appear as if the forces pressing down the roof accumulate in the columns, causing the columns to reflect this force by pushing the roof upwards. Therefore, the weight of this enormous roof is not apparent anywhere at *Muryangsu-jeon* Hall. The structure forgoes the use of ornamentation, and instead visually expresses the physical forces pressing down on the columns as a force that may bounce back upward. As a result, this has the effect of making it look as if the roof is floating in the air. This is the charm of *Muryangsu-jeon* Hall.

The ceiling of *Muryangsu-jeon* Hall appears to float in the air
공중에 떠 있는 것 같은 무량수전의 천장

무량수전의 백미, 배흘림기둥

더욱이 이 웅장한 건물에 비해 지나치게
굵지도 않고 가늘지도 않은 날씬한 기둥과
그 위에 올려진 마치 '산(山)'처럼 생긴 공포[06]
부재를 보면 그 하나하나가 마치 한 송이
꽃을 보는 느낌입니다. 마치 꽃이 지붕을
받치고 있는 모양 때문인지 그 지붕에서는
무게감이 전혀 느껴지지 않습니다. 그런데
무량수전의 기둥을 보면 중간 부분이

약간 볼록하게 부풀어 있습니다. 이것이
'배흘림기둥(entasis)' 양식입니다.
그런데 왜 이렇게 기둥을 깎았을까요? 이
기둥을 시각적으로만 보면 마치 위에서
아래로 내리누르는 힘 때문에 부푼 것처럼
보입니다. 일반적인 원통형 기둥이었다면
지붕이 내리누르는 힘이 기둥을 만나 절단된
느낌이 들었을지 모르지만, 배흘림기둥에는
그 힘이 일정한 압력으로 남아 있습니다.
거기에다 이렇게 팽팽하게 부풀었으니 그
힘을 금방이라도 튕겨낼 것만 같습니다.
무량수전의 건축가는 이처럼 지붕이
내리누르는 힘을 기둥에 축적시켰다가 그
반동으로 기둥이 지붕을 위로 밀어내는
것처럼 보이고자 했습니다. 그래서 우리는
무량수전 내부 어디에서도 이 거대한 지붕의
무게감을 느낄 수 없습니다.
장식을 극도로 배제하는 대신 내리누르는
물리적 힘을 도리어 위로 튕겨 올려보낼
것만 같은 시각적 힘으로 대체함으로써
지붕이 공중에 떠 있는 듯한 효과를 드러낸
것입니다. 이것이 부석사 무량수전만의
매력이라 하겠습니다.

• 06 Wooden parts of the framework that are cut and
     attached to support the weight of the eaves in
     traditional wooden structures.
     전통 목조 건축물에서 처마 끝의 하중을 받치기 위해
     짜 맞추어 댄 나무 부재.

If the entasis columns of *Muryangsu-jeon* Hall are considered flower stems, then the bracket sets above would be considered flowers, symbolizing that the hall has flowers supporting its roof.

무량수전의 배흘림기둥이 줄기라면 그 위의 공포는 꽃이다. 그래서 무량수전은 꽃이 지붕을 받치고 있는 것처럼 보인다.

스님용

Buseok-sa Temple, Modeled on Bodhgaya

The main Buddha in *Muryangsu-jeon* Hall is the Seated Clay Buddha Statue(National Treasure No. 45). While this clay statue was made during the Goryeo period, it is thought to have been created when Master Uisang first built Buseok-sa Temple, and since then has undergone continuous repairs. However, this Buddha statue, instead of facing the front of the sanctum, which is the common arrangement, faces the side of the building. That is, it is seated toward the west and faces east. A Buddha seated and facing east represents Sakyamuni Buddha, who gained enlightenment while watching the sun rise in the east from Bodhgaya. The statue features *Hangma Chokjiin*[07] of *Pyeondan Ugyeon*, which means the right shoulder is bare and one hand is touching the Earth(Earth-touching mudra or hand seal). This posture symbolizes *seongdo*(attaining Buddhahood or enlightenment) as Sakyamuni Buddha did. A Buddha with the same posture is also enshrined in Mahabodhi Temple in Bodhgaya, India. Interestingly, directly behind Mahabodhi Temple is the Vajra Throne or Indestructible Jeweled Seat(Vajrasana), said to be the rock on which Sakyamuni Buddha was seated at the time of his enlightenment. There is also an enormous rock behind the Buddha statue outside *Muryangsu-jeon* Hall at Buseok-sa Temple. This rock – which borrows its name from the temple itself – is called *Buseok*, or "floating rock."

This rock plays a key role in the story of Master Uisang and Seonmyo mentioned earlier. According to the story, Master Uisang wanted to build a temple here, but the site was occupied by non-Buddhists, preventing him from establishing a temple. Subsequently, Seonmyo, who had turned herself into a dragon, levitated this rock into the air and threatened to crush the non-Buddhists if they did not leave. This is the famous founding tale of Buseok-sa Temple.

Seated Clay Buddha Statue at Buseok-sa Temple, Yeongju
영주 부석사 소조여래좌상

Sakyamuni Buddha with the Earth-touching mudra (*Hangma Chokjiin*) at Mahabodhi Temple, Bodhgaya
보드가야 마하보디 사당의 항마성도상

보드가야를 모델로 했던 부석사

무량수전 중심에는 본존 불상인
소조여래좌상(국보 제45호)이 있습니다.
흙을 빚어 만든 이 불상은 고려시대에
만들어진 것이지만 의상 스님이 부석사를
창건하실 때 조성한 불상을 계속 수리해
온 것이 아닌가 추정되고 있습니다.
그런데 이 불상은 보통의 경우처럼
전각의 정면을 향하지 않고, 건물의 측면,
즉 서쪽에 앉아 동쪽을 향해 있습니다.
이처럼 동쪽을 향해 앉은 부처님은
보드가야에서 동쪽의 떠오르는 태양을
보며 깨달음을 얻으셨을 때의 석가모니
모습을 재현한 것입니다. 오른쪽 어깨를
드러내고 오른손으로 땅을 가리키고
있음을 의미하는 편단우견(偏袒右肩)의
항마촉지인(降魔觸地印)[07]의 모습은 바로
석가모니불의 성도(成道)를 상징하는
자세입니다. 실제 인도 보드가야의
마하보디 사당에도 이와 같은 자세의
부처님이 모셔져 있지요.

흥미로운 점은 마하보디 사당 바로 뒤에
석가모니불께서 깨달음을 얻으실 당시
앉으셨던 돌인 금강보좌(金剛寶座)가 자리
잡고 있는데, 부석사 무량수전 불상의 뒤편
바깥에도 거대한 바위가 자리 잡고 있다는
점입니다. 이 바위가 부석사 이름 속의
부석(浮石), 즉 '떠 있는 돌'입니다.
이 돌에는 앞서 말씀드린 의상 스님과
선묘의 이야기가 담겨 있습니다.
이야기인즉 의상 스님께서 처음 이곳에
절을 짓고자 하셨으나 외도들이 먼저
들어와 있어 터를 잡을 수 없게 되었습니다.
그러자 용으로 변한 선묘가 이 돌을
공중에 띄워 외도들에게 떠나지 않으면
떨어뜨리겠다고 위협해 쫓아냈다는
것입니다. 이 이야기는 부석사의 창건
설화로 유명합니다.

07   Earth-touching(Bhumi-sparsa) mudra or hand
     gesture symbolizing Sakyamuni Buddha's proof
     of his enlightenment by the god of Earth, thereby
     destroying demons.
     석가모니께서 마군들을 항복시키기 위해 땅의 신을
     불러내실 때의 모습으로서 석가모니의 성불을
     상징하는 대표적인 자세.

The floating rock preserving the legend
of Buseok-sa Temple
부석사의 전설을 간직한 부석

The Lingering Presence of Master Uisang

If one climbs the tranquil mountain path that passes between the Three-story Stone Pagoda(Treasure No. 249) and *Muryangsu-jeon* Hall, you will arrive at *Josa-dang* or Shrine of Patriarchs(National Treasure No. 19) where there is a special tree. Its name is *Seonbihwa*, and this is where Master Uisang thrust a cane into the ground while entering Nirvana; it later sprouted and became a tree. This story is told in *Taengniji* by Lee Junghwan.[08] The tree is a Chinese peashrub and appears rather feeble, but it is believed to be about 1,350 years old. The reason

Master Uisang modeled Buseok-sa Temple on Bodhgaya is because the *Flower Ornament Sutra* is based on the moment when Sakyamuni Buddha attained enlightenment in Bodhgaya. From this perspective, *Seonbihwa* symbolizes the Bodhi tree, a symbol for Bodhgaya. The name *Seonbihwa* means "a tree that enters *Seon*(Chan in Chinese and Zen in Japanese)." Therefore, it is regarded as the tree of enlightenment.

There is one more site not to be missed if you visit Buseok-sa Temple, and it can be seen from the low hill where the

Josa-dang at Buseok-sa Temple
영주 부석사 조사당

Three-story Stone Pagoda is built. The view that extends out from the Sobaek-san Mountain range far away makes one feel as if nature is rushing into Buseok-sa Temple in order to meet Master Uisang; it is like encountering 100 billion Buddhas, Bodhisattvas, and gods advancing to praise the enlightenment of Buddha as told in the *Flower Ornament Sutra*.

Even though Master Uisang resided in a temple in the mountains, he did not turn his back on the world. When King Munmu[09] announced the construction of a new capital city, the Master wrote him and requested that he not put such a burden on the people. He also exchanged letters with Master Fazang, whom he had studied with under Great Master Zhiyan. If Bodhgaya was the center of enlightenment, Buseok-sa Temple was the center of the Flower Ornament School in East Asia. In *Samguk Yusa*(Legends and History of Korea's Three Kingdoms), Master Ilyeon[10] praised Master Uisang as follows.

Through the forest, across the ocean, beyond the clouds of dust, The gates of Jisang-sa Temple opened and welcomed this treasure. After digging up the essence of the Flower Ornament and planting it on our soil to bloom, Spring came to Mt. Zhongnan and Mt. Taebaek-san.

Here, Master Ilyeon used the term "dig up," and it was meant literally. India and Silla were able to become one because Master Uisang excavated the Vajra Throne, the Bodhi tree, and the Buddha statue with Earth-touching mudra representing the attainment of enlightenment and planted them in Korea to flourish.

아직 남아 있는 의상 스님의 향기

무량수전 옆의 삼층석탑(보물 제249호)
사이로 난 고즈넉한 산길을 따라
조사당(국보 제19호)에 오르면 특별한 나무를
만나게 됩니다. 이중환[08]의 『택리지』에서도
언급한바 의상 스님이 입적하시면서 꽂아둔
지팡이에서 싹이나 도로 나무가 되었다는
'선비화(禪扉花)'가 그 주인공입니다.
원래는 골담초라는 나무인데, 보기에는
가냘퍼도 무려 1,350여 년을 살아온
나무입니다. 의상 스님이 부석사를
인도의 보드가야를 본떠 만드신 이유는

바로 『화엄경』의 배경이 석가모니께서
보드가야에서 깨달음을 막 이룬 순간이었기
때문인데, 그렇게 본다면 보드가야를
대표하는 상징인 보리수의 역할을
이 선비화가 대신하는 셈입니다.
이름부터가 '선(禪)으로 들어가는 나무',
즉 깨달음의 나무이니까요.
부석사에 들르신다면 놓치지 말아야 할
또 하나의 장면이 있습니다. 삼층석탑이
세워진 얕은 구릉에서 바라보는 풍광이
그것입니다. 멀리 소백산맥으로부터

펼쳐지는 풍광은 마치 자연조차도 의상
스님을 뵙기 위해 부석사로 몰려오는 것
같은 기분을 들게 합니다. 『화엄경』에서
부처님의 깨달음을 찬탄하기 위해 몰려든 온
우주의 백만억 불보살들과 천신들을 대하는
듯합니다.

비록 산중의 사찰에 계신 의상 스님이셨지만
세상을 등진 것은 아니었습니다. 스님은
문무왕'09이 도성을 새로 건설하겠다고
하자 편지를 써 백성들을 수고롭게 하지 말
것을 부탁하기도 했고, 지엄 문하에서 함께
공부하던 법장 스님과도 편지를 주고받으며
세상과 소통했습니다. 깨달음의 중심에
보드가야가 있었다면, 동아시아 화엄종의
중심에는 이처럼 부석사가 있었던 것입니다.
『삼국유사』에서 일연 스님'10은
의상 스님을 다음과 같이 칭송했습니다.

披榛跨海冒煙塵
至相門開接瑞珍
采采雜花我故國
終南太伯一般春

숲길 헤치고 바다 건너 흙먼지를 지나니
지상사의 문이 열려 이 보배를 맞이했네
화엄을 통째로 캐어다가 우리 땅에 꽃피우니
종남산과 태백산이 일시에 봄을 맞이했네

여기서 일연 스님은 '캐오다[采]'라는
표현을 썼는데 정말 그랬습니다.
의상 스님께서 인도 보드가야의 금강보좌,
보리수, 그리고 항마성도의 불상을 캐어다
우리나라에 심어 꽃피운 덕분에 인도와
신라는 그렇게 하나가 되었습니다.

•08   1690-1752. A scholar who lived in the late
      Joseon period. His best known writing is
      Taengniji, a study of geography, sociology, and
      economics, written while traveling all over the
      country.
      1690-1752. 조선 후기의 학자. 대표 저술로
      전국을 다니면서 지리·사회·경제를 연구한
      『택리지』가 있다.

•09   626-681. 30th King of Silla.
      626-681. 신라 제30대 왕.

•10   1206-1289. A monk of Goryeo and the author
      of *Samguk Yusa*.
      1206-1289. 고려시대 승려. 삼국시대의 역사와
      전설을 다룬 『삼국유사』의 저자이다.

◁ *Seonbihwa* at *Josa-dang*, Buseok-sa Temple
부석사 조사당 선비화

Bongjeong-sa Temple

in Andong City

안 동

봉정사

The Layout of Bongjeong-sa Temple
봉정사 가람 배치도

1	*Manse-ru* 만세루
2	*Beomjong-gak* 범종각
3	Seongbo Museum 성보박물관
4	*Gogeum-dang* 고금당
5	*Hwaeom Gangdang* 화엄강당
6	*Muryanghaehoe* 무량해회
7	*Daeung-jeon* 대웅전
8	*Geungnak-jeon* 극락전
9	*Samseong-gak* 삼성각
10	Yeongsan-am Hermitage 영산암

Architecture as a Living Museum

살아있는 건축 박물관

Hahoe Village in Andong is designated as a UNESCO World Heritage Site. Historical buildings are not only located in Hahoe Village, but are also hidden all throughout the city of Andong. Many of these old buildings still remain today, which is a testament to how much Andong residents revere and protect tradition.

In the text of *Taengniji*, Lee Junghwan stated there was a Silla temple located north of *Yeongho-ru*, a well-known pavilion in Andong. Lee writes:

Although the temple has been abandoned and the monks have left, the main hall stands solid and alone in a field with no sign of tilting. Hence, people compare it to Linguang Hall in Lu.

Linguang of Lu was a hall built within the royal palace in the state of Lu during the Han Dynasty. It is often used as a metaphor for splendid and exceptional architecture. There is a strong possibility that the temple he spoke of located north of *Yeongho-ru* in Andong was Bongjeong-sa Temple.

Bongjeong-sa Temple contains the oldest wooden architecture in Korea. *Geungnak-jeon* Hall, which is now known to date from the Goryeo period, was originally considered to date from the Silla period. That mistake is understandable given that *Geungnak-jeon* Hall has also been evaluated as featuring architectural elements characteristic of the Three Kingdoms period, despite being built during the Goryeo period. If so, that means Master Uisang may have touched the same old temple pillars that we can touch today.

Bongjeong-sa Temple was built in 672, either by Master Uisang or his disciple, Master Neungin. Both propositions imply that the temple was an extension of Master Uisang's *Avatamsaka Sutra* School, or School of the *Flower Ornament Sutra*. It also appears that Biro-sa Temple in Punggi, located near Buseok-sa Temple, was established by Master Jinjeong, also Master Uisang's disciple. Therefore, it is likely that temples built by disciples of Master Uisang were located in the Yeongju, Andong, and Punggi areas.

안동에는 이미 세계문화유산에 이름을 올린 하회마을이 있습니다. 그런 안동에는 하회마을에만 있을 법한 고택이 곳곳에 숨어 있습니다. 이렇게 오래된 건축물들이 많이 남아 있는 것은 그만큼 안동 사람들이 전통을 중요하게 생각하고 지켜 왔기 때문일 것입니다.

한편 조선 후기 지리학자 이중환은 『택리지』에서 안동의 대표적인 누각이었던 영호루 북쪽에 신라 시대의 절이 있다고 하였습니다.

지금은 절이 망해 스님은 없어도 그 정전은 들 복판에 따로 서 있어 조금도 기울지 않아 사람들이 노나라의 영광전(靈光殿)에 견준다.

'노나라 영광전'이란 한(漢)나라 때 노(魯)나라 지역에 세워졌던 궁궐 전각의 이름입니다. 화려하고 훌륭한 건축물의 비유로 종종 쓰이지요. 안동 영호루 북쪽의 이 절은 봉정사였을 가능성이 매우 높습니다.

봉정사는 우리나라에서 가장 오래된 목조 건축물이 있는 사찰로서 지금은 고려시대의 전각으로 알려진 극락전과 같은 건축물이 이때만 해도 신라의 건축물로 간주되어 왔던 것을 알 수 있습니다. 물론 이는 지금의 시각에서 보더라도 결코 허황한 해석이 아닙니다. 고려시대 건축으로 알려진 극락전은 양식적으로는 삼국시대 건축의 특징을 지니고 있는 것으로 평가되고 있기 때문입니다. 만약 그렇다면 우리의 손길이 닿는 극락전의 오래된 기둥에 의상 스님께서도 손을 짚으셨을 수 있다는 이야기가 됩니다.

봉정사는 672년에 의상 스님이 세웠다고도 하고, 스님의 제자 능인 스님이 세웠다고도 합니다. 결국 의상 스님의 화엄종의 연장선상에 있었던 절이라는 뜻입니다. 부석사 인근의 풍기 비로사도 의상 스님의 제자인 진정 스님이 창건했다는 것으로 보아 영주와 안동, 풍기 인근에 의상 스님의 제자들이 창건한 절이 포진해 있었을 가능성은 충분합니다.

Bongjeong-sa Temple and Yeongsan-am Hermitage, Andong
안동 봉정사와 영산암

Passing through *Manse-ru* Pavilion

Passing through the temple's One Pillar Gate, you stand under the stairs leading up to *Manse-ru* Pavilion. However, from outside the temple *Manse-ru* Pavilion is hardly visible through the large trees growing in front of it. Also, the entrance under *Manse-ru* Pavilion is so small that you might question whether this is the actual entrance. Indeed, such a diminutive entrance is rare for a temple.

Pavilions at other temples often feature a relatively large door or an open space, but Bongjeong-sa's pavilion is closed off by embankments. The entrance to *Manse-ru* Pavilion looks even narrower because of the naturally curved tree trunk used for the door sill, and the door jambs resemble the front entrance of a private home. The passage is so narrow that only one person can pass through with ease, but larger objects or groups of people would be a problem. The narrow entrance seems to symbolize that beyond the door is a world completely different and isolated from this world.

However, measuring five *kan*s across in front, the actual size of *Manse-ru* Pavilion is not small. Beyond the narrow gate, you must go through a long passageway that resembles a tunnel in order to enter the temple grounds. The ceiling of the tunnel is in fact the floor of the pavilion, and the floor is so wide that it forms a long tunnel-like entrance. If you look at *Manse-ru* Pavilion from the temple grounds, you can get a sense of how big it is.

Mandae-ru Pavilion at Byeongsan-Seowon(a traditional Confucian Academy) in Andong is typical of Korean pavilion architecture. In fact, both *Mandae-ru* and *Manse-ru* Pavilions are two outstanding works of architecture that feature the architectural style of Andong. However, while *Mandae-ru* was only for Confucian scholars and aristocrats, *Manse-ru* was a place for all sentient beings.

Manse-ru, Bongjeong-sa, Andong
안동 봉정사 만세루

An entrance below *Manse-ru* Pavilion in Bongjeong-sa Temple
봉정사 만세루 하단의 입구

만세루를 지나며

일주문을 지나 봉정사 만세루로 이어지는 계단 아래에 섭니다. 그런데 이 만세루는 그 앞에 자란 커다란 나무들에 가려 잘 보이지 않습니다. 또 만세루 아래의 입구도 작아서 이곳으로 들어가는 것이 맞는지 망설여지기도 합니다. 입구가 이렇듯 비밀스럽게 숨어 있는 절도 드물지요. 다른 절의 만세루는 아래로 비교적 넓은 문이 있거나 공간이 개방되어 있는데, 이곳은 축대로 막혀 있습니다. 봉정사 만세루의 문이 더욱 좁아 보이는 이유는 둥글게 휜 나무를 자연스레 문지방으로 쓰고, 옆에는 문설주까지 세워 살림집 대문처럼 만들었기 때문입니다. 한 사람쯤이야 그냥 들어간다지만 이렇게 좁은 통로여서야 다른 짐이나 대중들은 어떻게 드나들었을까 싶습니다. 그만큼 이 문 너머는 이 세상과 격리된 전혀 다른 세계라는 것을 상징적으로 보여주는 것 같습니다.

하지만 만세루의 실제 규모는 정면 5칸으로 결코 작지 않습니다. 좁은 문 안으로 들어서면 마치 터널처럼 긴 공간을 통과해 경내로 들어가야 하는데, 터널의 천장 부분이 실은 누각의 마루입니다. 그만큼 마루가 넓어 긴 터널형의 진입로가 형성된 것입니다. 만세루를 경내에서 바라보면 얼마나 넓고 큰 누각인지 실감이 갑니다. 우리나라 누각을 대표하는 건축물 중의 하나가 인근에 있는 안동 병산서원(屛山書院)의 만대루(晩對樓)입니다. 봉정사의 만세루는 실로 그와 쌍벽을 이루는 누각입니다. 이 두 누각은 그야말로 '안동 양식'이라 할 만한 공통점을 지녔습니다. 그러나 만대루가 오로지 유생과 양반을 위한 공간이라면 이 만세루는 모든 중생들을 위한 공간이었습니다.

Daeung-jeon, Bongjeong-sa Temple, Andong. Like *Daeung-jeon* Hall at Bongjeong-sa Temple, the technique of placing a sturdy, wooden lintel between two columns and then placing more *gongpo* on top of it is referred to as *dapo*.
안동 봉정사 대웅전. 봉정사 대웅전처럼 기둥과 기둥 사이에 튼튼한 나무 부재를 얹어 그 위에 더 많은 공포를 얹는 방식을 '다포(多包)'라고 한다.

The Relationship of *Daeung-jeon* Hall to King Gongmin

After passing *Manse-ru* Pavilion, you will reach the magnificent temple hall named *Daeung-jeon*(National Treasure No. 311). *Daeung-jeon* in Bongjeong-sa Temple is a structure with a hip-and-gable roof and is typical of early *dapo*-style[01] architecture in Korea. It is characterized by long eaves as wooden buildings are vulnerable to rain damage. In order to support these eaves, a unique device called a *gongpo* was developed, which stretches out from the wall like an arm to support the eaves. When the *gongpo* is on top of a column, it is referred to as a *jusimpo*.[02] Like *Daeung-jeon* Hall at Bongjeong-sa Temple, the technique of placing a sturdy, wooden lintel between two columns and then placing more *gongpo* on top of it is referred to as *dapo*, a style that emerged after *jusimpo*. One example of early *dapo*-style architecture is *Namdae-mun* Gate in Seoul. Its complex brackets resemble those used on Bongjeong-sa Temple's *Daeung-jeon* Hall. Hence, the *Daeung-jeon* Hall at Bongjeong-sa Temple is also regarded as an example of early Joseon architecture. However, in 1997, a mural painting of

the Vulture Peak Assembly(Treasure No. 1614) was discovered when the Amitabha Buddha Dharma Talk Painting(Treasure No. 1643) hanging in *Daeung-jeon* Hall was removed for repair. The style of the mural resembled Goryeo Buddhist paintings, presenting the possibility it dated from the Goryeo period. Consequently, if the mural is from the Goryeo period, then the date of *Daeung-jeon*'s construction may also date back to that period.

Subsequent to this discovery, *Daeung-jeon* Hall was dismantled and repaired in 1999, and a previously unseen statement written in ink was found under the Buddhist altar which read, "repaired Buddhist altar in 1361." This confirms that the building's decorations, including the altar, were created at least before 1361. All the evidence indicates that Bongjeong-sa's *Daeung-jeon* Hall was built in the Goryeo period.

How did the first *dapo*-type building in Korea come to be built in Andong? The answer can be found in stories about King Gongmin who fled to Andong in 1361 to escape the Red Turban Rebellion[03] at

●01 *Dapo*: multi-bracket style.

●02 *Jusimpo*: column-head style.

A mural painting of the Vulture Peak Assembly, Bongjeong–sa, Andong
안동 봉정사 영산회상벽화

the end of the Goryeo period. At the time that King Gongmin[04] fled, the people of Andong helped him and his family, who were in despair. They even carried Queen Noguk Daejang[05] across the river on their shoulders and provided full material and moral support.

Thus, King Gongmin, who later returned to Gaeseong, promoted the village to the status of *Andong-Daedohobu*(specialized government administrative area) and sent many gifts.

Two of these are the name plaque, '*Andong-Ungbu*(安東雄府),' that hangs on the door of the government office of *Andong-Dohobu*, and the name plaque of *Yeongho-ru*, Andong's well-known pavilion, written by King Gongmin himself. The name plaque on *Muryangsu-jeon*(無量壽殿) Hall at Buseok-sa Temple, discussed

The Amitabha Buddha Dharma Talk Painting, Bongjeong-sa, Andong
안동 봉정사 아미타설법도

earlier, is also said to be the calligraphy of King Gongmin, indicating his keen interest in the area. The name plaque on '*Jinyeomun*(眞如門)' at Bongjeong-sa Temple is also said to be his calligraphy. Hence, it may be assumed that *dapo*-type architecture, then a recent import from the Yuan Dynasty, was built by top architects of Gaeseong who followed King Gongmin when he fled here.

The interior of *Daeung-jeon* Hall was also decorated in a new style. The ceiling was flattened by weaving square wooden boards called *wumulbanja*, which were painted with lotus mandalas. The inside of *Daeung-jeon* Hall is literally a "World of the Lotus Treasury" filled with lotus flowers. Also, a pair of dragons slither up the pillars supporting the Buddhist altar, creating a dynamic atmosphere.

공민왕과의 인연이 깃든 대웅전

만세루를 지나 마주하게 되는 웅장한
전각은 대웅전(국보 제311호)입니다.
봉정사 대웅전은 우리나라 초기 다포
건축을 대표하는 팔작지붕의 건축물입니다.
목조 건축물은 아무래도 비에 약하기
때문에 처마를 길게 빼는 것이 특징입니다.
이 처마를 받치기 위해 공포(栱包)라는
독특한 부재가 등장했는데 말하자면
벽체로부터 팔을 내밀어서 처마를 받쳐주는
역할을 하는 것입니다. 이 공포가 기둥
위에만 있으면 '주심포(柱心包)'라 하고,
봉정사 대웅전처럼 기둥과 기둥 사이에
튼튼한 나무 부재(平枋)를 얹어 그 위에
더 많은 공포를 얹는 방식을 주심포보다
나중에 등장한 '다포(多包)'라고 합니다.
초기 다포 건축물로는 조선 초기의 서울
남대문이 있는데, 봉정사 대웅전의 포와
서로 닮아 봉정사 대웅전도 조선 초기
건축물로 간주되었습니다.
그런데 1997년 대웅전에 걸려 있던
아미타설법도(보물 제1643호)를 수리하기
위해 떼어내자 그 안에 숨겨져 있던
영산회상벽화(보물 제1614호)가 모습을
드러내었습니다. 이 벽화는 그림의 양식이
고려불화의 화풍과 닮아서 고려시대
벽화일 가능성이 제기되었습니다. 물론
벽화가 고려시대 것이라면 건물도 그만큼

시대를 올려볼 수 있게 됩니다. 그러다
1999년 대웅전을 해체·수리하면서 불단
아래 '1361년에 불단을 수리했다'는 뜻밖의
묵서명이 발견되었습니다. 최소한 불단을
비롯한 내부의 장엄이 1361년 이전에
만들어진 것이 확인되었기 때문에 결국
대웅전의 건축 연대도 고려시대로 올려볼
증거를 찾게 된 셈입니다.
그렇다면 우리나라 최초의 다포계 건축물이
왜 이곳 안동에 세워지게 되었을까요?
해답은 고려 말 홍건적의 난[03]을 피해
1361년 안동으로 피신 왔던 공민왕[04]의
행적에서 찾을 수 있습니다. 몽진 당시
안동에서 급박하게 냇물을 건너는데
주민들이 물에 들어가 어깨를 맞대어
노국대장공주[05]를 건너게 해 주는 등
실의에 빠져 있던 공민왕 일행을 안동
사람들이 물심양면 도왔다고 전합니다.
그래서 개성으로 돌아간 공민왕은 이곳을
안동대도호부로 승격시키고 많은 선물을
남겼습니다. 그 흔적이 바로 안동도호부
관아에 걸었던 공민왕의 친필 현판
"안동웅부"와 안동 대표 누각인 영호루의
현판입니다. 앞서 살펴본 부석사 무량수전
현판 역시 공민왕의 글씨라 전하여 이
근방에 대한 공민왕의 관심이 지대했음을
보여주고 있습니다. 마찬가지로 봉정사에

The ceiling of *Daeung-jeon* Hall is filled with lotus mandalas.
대웅전 천장은 연꽃 만다라로 가득하다.

전하는 "진여문" 현판 역시 공민왕의
글씨로 전합니다. 아마도 당시 공민왕의
몽진을 따라왔던 개성의 일급 건축가들에
의해 원나라에서 막 수입된 다포계 건축이
봉정사에 세워진 것 아닌가 보고 있습니다.
대웅전의 내부도 새로운 개념으로
장엄되었습니다. 천장은 '우물반자'라고
부르는 네모난 나무판들을 엮어 평평하게
만들었습니다. 그리고 그 안에 가득
연꽃 만다라를 그렸습니다. 대웅전
내부를 그야말로 연꽃으로 가득한
연화장세계(蓮華藏世界)로 표현한 것입니다.

또한 불단을 지탱하는 두 기둥에는 용이
휘감고 올라가는 모습을 그려 넣어 더욱
역동적입니다.

- 03 A rebellion by peasants which occurred in the
  midlands at the end of the Yuan Dynasty in China.
  It served as a starting point for the founding of the
  Ming Dynasty. Some of the rebel groups invaded
  Goryeo through Manchuria when they were chased
  by Yuan Dynasty troops.
  중국 원나라 말기에 중원에서 발생하여 명나라
  건국의 계기가 된 농민반란. 반란을 일으킨 무리가
  원나라의 추격을 받자 일부가 만주를 거쳐 고려에도
  침입하였다.

- 04 1330-1374. 31st King of Goryeo.
  1330-1374. 고려 제31대 왕.

- 05 ?-1365. King Gongmin's queen, a princess from the
  Yuan Dynasty.
  ?-1365. 공민왕의 왕비.

Mural Hidden Behind Buddhist Painting

불화 뒤에 숨은 벽화

The historical text *Beopdang Jungchanggi*(record of Dharma Hall restoration) was also discovered in Bongjeong-sa's *Daeung-jeon* Hall. This text says that in 1428 during the reign of King Sejong, "*Mireukhasaengdo*, the Descent of Maitreya Buddha was drawn, and in 1435 a pavilion with two halls was constructed." If the term *Mireukhasaengdo* refers to the picture hanging in *Daeung-jeon* Hall, then the mural below it must have been painted at least before 1428. The mural is a work of outstanding artistic merit. Unfortunately, all the faces of the figures in the mural had been scratched out. The reason for this is unknown, but that damage may have led to the overlay of a new Buddhist painting during the reign of King Sejong.

봉정사 대웅전에서는 「법당중창기」도 발견되었습니다. 여기에는 세종 때인 1428년에 '미륵하생도를 그리고, 1435년에 이당(二堂) 전각을 조성했다'고 씌여 있었습니다. 만약 '미륵하생도'가 대웅전에 걸린 그림이라면 최소한 그 아래의 벽화는 1428년 이전에 그려진 것이 됩니다.
이 벽화는 매우 뛰어난 작품이지만 아쉽게도 벽화 속 존상들의 얼굴이 모두 날카로운 것으로 긁혀 훼손되었습니다. 원인은 모르지만 바로 이 훼손 때문에 부득이 세종 때 새로 불화를 그려 넣어야 했을지도 모릅니다.

Geungnak-jeon Hall, the Oldest Wooden Building in Korea

Geungnak-jeon Hall(National Treasure No. 15) is the Dharma hall standing next to *Daeung-jeon*.

The layout of Bongjeong-sa Temple is characterized by the arrangement of *Daeung-jeon* that enshrines Sakyamuni Buddha, and it is located next to *Geungnak-jeon* Hall that enshrines Amitabha Buddha. This arrangement is similar to how *Geungnak-jeon* Hall stands one level below *Daeung-jeon* at Bulguk-sa Temple. Such an arrangement is often found at Buddhist temples established by Master Uisang and his disciples. Perhaps

Master Uisang continued the tradition of placing great importance on Amitabha Buddha, despite his being a follower of the *Hwaeom* School(School of the *Avatamsaka Sutra*).

One record says that *Geungnak-jeon* Hall had its roof repaired in 1363, indicating it was built at least before then. Unlike the temple's *Daeung-jeon* Hall, which is presumed to be from the Goryeo period, *Geungnak-jeon* Hall has architectural features that date back to the Three Kingdoms period. The most prominent characteristics are two components known

Geungnak-jeon Hall at Bongjeong-sa Temple
안동 봉정사 극락전

as *soseul hapjang* and *bokhwaban*. A *soseul hapjang*, such as the one in *Geungnak-jeon* Hall, traverses the entire roof of a structure and is an old feature only seen up until the Tang Dynasty in China. The *bokhwaban* can only be seen in the oldest wooden structure in China, Nanchan Temple's Great Buddha Hall in Shanxi Province. In Korea, there are traces of similar elements in murals found in Goguryeo tombs. Hence, the building that preserves the *bokhwaban* used during the Three Kingdoms period is indeed a living relic. There is another reason to view Bongjeong-sa Temple's *Geungnak-jeon* Hall as the oldest wooden building in Korea. *Geungnak-jeon* Hall is an example of *jusimpo*-style architecture

in which complex brackets are situated directly above each column. However, its composition style is simpler than other Goryeo buildings that have *jusimpo*-style architecture, such as Buseok-sa Temple's *Muryangsu-jeon* Hall and Sudeok-sa Temple's *Daeung-jeon* Hall in Yesan County. Therefore, it can be seen as the original and standard form of *jusimpo*-style architecture.

Geungnak-jeon looks simple on the outside, but its ceiling structure inside is extremely complicated. If the ceiling of Buseok-sa Temple's *Muryangsu-jeon* Hall appears to be floating in air, Bongjeong-sa Temple's *Geungnak-jeon* Hall feels like it is comfortably embracing anyone standing inside it.

① A *Soseul hapjang*
소슬합장

② A *Bokhwaban*
복화반

Inside of *Geungnak-jeon* Hall
극락전 내부

우리나라에서 가장 오래된 목조 건축물, 극락전

대웅전과 나란하게 서 있는 법당은 극락전(국보 제15호)입니다. 석가모니불을 모신 대웅전과 아미타불을 모신 극락전이 나란히 있는 것이 봉정사 가람 배치의 특징입니다. 불국사에서 대웅전 옆으로 한 단 아래에 극락전이 위치한 것과 유사한데, 이러한 배치는 의상 스님과 그 제자 스님들의 사찰에서 자주 나타나는 형식이기도 합니다. 아마도 의상 스님이 화엄종파이면서도 아미타불을 중요시했던 전통을 계승한 것으로 보입니다.

극락전은 1363년에 지붕을 중수했다는 기록이 있어 최소한 이 이전에 세워진 전각임이 밝혀졌습니다. 그런데 고려시대의 것으로 추정되는 대웅전과 달리 극락전은 삼국시대까지 거슬러 올라갈 수 있는 건축적 특징이 있는데, 가장 대표적인 것이 '소슬합장'과 '복화반'이라 부르는 부재입니다. 극락전에서처럼 지붕 전체를 가로지르는 소슬합장은 중국에서도 당나라 때까지만 보이는 오래된 특징이고, 복화반은 중국에서 가장 오래된 목조 건축물인 산서성 남선사(南禪寺) 대전에서나 볼 수 있습니다. 우리나라에서는 고구려 고분벽화의 그림에서 이와 유사한 부재의 흔적을 찾아볼 수 있습니다. 이렇듯 까마득한 삼국시대에 사용되었던 복화반이 사용된 건물이 실제 남아 있으니 그야말로 살아 있는 화석인 셈입니다.

봉정사 극락전을 우리나라에서 가장 오래된 목조 건물로 보는 또 하나의 이유가 있습니다. 극락전은 기둥 위에만 포가 있는 주심포식 건축물인데 같은 고려시대 주심포 건축물이라도 부석사 무량수전이나 예산 수덕사 대웅전에 비해 더 단순하고 간결한 구성을 보이고 있기 때문입니다. 이는 주심포 형식의 표준이자 가장 시원적인 형태로 볼 수 있습니다.

극락전은 겉에서 보기에는 단출하지만 안으로 들어가 보면 천장의 구조가 매우 복잡합니다. 부석사 무량수전의 천장이 공중에 떠 있는 느낌이라면, 봉정사 극락전은 안에 있는 사람을 포근히 감싸는 느낌으로 다가옵니다.

Hwaeom Gangdang, a Wing Bracket-style Work of Architecture

The pavilion forming a T-shape with *Geungnak-jeon* Hall and *Daeung-jeon* Hall is *Hwaeom Gangdang*(Treasure No. 448). This lecture hall, where the *Flower Ornament Sutra* is taught, is an important building that tells us Bongjeong-sa Temple follows the doctrine of the *Hwaeom* School. Its simple antique ornamental painting design and gable roof, and its limited use of brackets on columns are similar to *Geungnak-jeon*, but there are slight differences in the complex brackets. The difference is that the bracket does not go on the top of the pillar like *jusimpo*, but the components are inserted into the column and installed in conjunction. Its curve resembles a seagull's wing, which is why it is referred to as *ikkong*-style, using the Chinese character 翼(*ik*), meaning wing.

The advantage of *ikkong*-style architecture lies in the interlocking of complex brackets and columns that can effectively withstand external shock. The *Hwaeom Gangdang* is classified as a transitional style that shows the progression from the complex column-top bracket style to wing bracket style. The *Hwaeom Gangdang* was restored in 1588. Therefore, it was probably built earlier during the Joseon period. At the center of Bongjeong-sa Temple are *Daeung-jeon* Hall, *Geungnak-jeon* Hall, and *Hwaeom Gangdang*. While *Geungnak-jeon* Hall features early *jusimpo*-style and *Daeung-jeon* Hall features early *dapo*-style, the *Hwaeom Gangdang* reveals the first appearance of the complex wing bracket-style. Bongjeong-sa Temple is literally an architectural museum where one can see early forms of all architectural techniques in one place.

Hwaeom gangdang at Bongjeong-sa Temple, Andong
안동 봉정사 화엄강당

Gongpo of *Hwaeom gangdang* resembles a seagull's wing, which is why it is referred to as *ikkong*-style.
화엄강당의 공포는 갈매기의 날개를 닮아 익공식이라 부른다.

익공식 건축물, 화엄강당

극락전·대웅전과 '丁'자형을 이루며 놓인 전각은 화엄강당(보물 제448호)입니다. '화엄을 강론하는 법당'이므로 봉정사가 화엄종 사찰임을 웅변하는 중요한 건축물입니다. 고졸한 단청, 단순 명쾌한 맞배지붕, 그리고 기둥 위에만 포가 있다는 점에서 극락전과 비슷하지만 공포는 조금 다릅니다. 주심포처럼 기둥 머리 위에 포가 올라가는 것이 아니라, 부재가 기둥 일부를 파고 들어와 기둥과 맞물려 설치된다는 게 차이입니다. 이것이 갈매기 날개처럼 휘어 있어서 날개 익(翼) 자를 써 '익공식'으로 불립니다. 익공식 건축은 공포가 기둥과 더 강하게 맞물려 외부 충격에 효과적으로 대응할 수 있다는 점이 장점입니다. 화엄강당은 주심포에서 이러한 익공식으로 넘어가는 과정을 보여주는 과도기 형식으로 분류됩니다.

화엄강당은 1588년에 중수한 것이 밝혀져 실제 지어진 것은 이보다 이른 조선 초기였을 것입니다. 결국 봉정사의 중심은 대웅전, 극락전, 화엄강당 세 채의 전각인데, 극락전은 가장 초기의 주심포 형식을 대변하고, 대웅전은 가장 초기의 다포 형식을 대변한다면, 화엄강당은 익공식 공포가 태어나는 과정을 보여주고 있는 것입니다. 봉정사는 그야말로 모든 건축 기법의 초기 형식을 한 경내에서 볼 수 있는 건축박물관인 셈입니다.

Gogeumdang and *Muryanghaehoe*, the Living Quarters of Bongjeong-sa

The building west of *Geungnak-jeon* Hall is called *Gogeum-dang*(Treasure No. 449), meaning "Old Golden Hall." Although the building is relatively small in size, records show that it used a similar wing bracket-style as at the *Hwaeom Gangdang* and was reconstructed in 1616 during the reign of King Gwanghaegun.[06]

Although it is now used as a *yosachae*(residence for monks), it is possible that the pavilion used to be the main Buddha hall of Bongjeong-sa Temple, as its name indicates that it was formerly a "Golden Hall."[07] This means the original centerline of Bongjeong-sa Temple was not a north-south axis as it is now, but an east-west axis with *Gogeum-dang* facing east. This is reminiscent of *Muryangsu-jeon* Hall at Buseok-sa Temple where the enshrined Buddha statue faces east. Could this be another characteristic of Master Uisang's Flower Ornament School Temples?

If *Gogeumdang* on the grounds of *Geungnak-jeon* is the right wing, then another *yosachae* named *Muryanghaehoe* on the grounds of *Daeung-jeon* is the left wing of Bongjeong-sa Temple. *Muryanghaehoe* is a residential building as luxurious as the old houses of Hahoe Village. In fact, renowned scholars from Andong, including Toegye Yi Hwang,[08] visited the temple. At that time it may have been a building used for guests. The wooden floor outside the *yosachae* is exquisite.

Gogeum-dang at Bongjeong-sa Temple, Andong
안동 봉정사 고금당

Muryanghaehoe at Bongjeong-sa Temple, Andong
안동 봉정사 무량해회

봉정사의 요사채, 고금당·무량해회

극락전 영역의 서쪽 전각은 옛 금당이란 의미의 '고금당(古金堂, 보물 제449호)'입니다. 크기는 비교적 작은 건물이지만 그 기법을 보면 화엄강당과 유사한 익공식 건축물로 광해군[06] 때인 1616년에 중수된 기록이 있습니다.

지금은 요사채이지만 전각의 이름이 '옛 금당[07]'인 것으로 보아 과거에는 봉정사의 주불전이 있던 자리였을 가능성도 있습니다. 그렇다면 원래의 봉정사 중심선은 지금처럼 남북 축선이 아니라 고금당이 바라보는 동쪽 축선이었다는 이야기가 됩니다. 이와 비슷하게 전각 안의 불상이 동쪽을 향해 봉안된 부석사 무량수전이 연상됩니다. 이 역시 의상 대사의 화엄사찰이 지닌 특징이었을까요?

극락전 영역에서 고금당이 오른쪽 날개를 이룬다면 대웅전 영역에서는 '무량해회(無量海會)'라는 요사채가 왼쪽 날개를 이루며 펼쳐집니다. 이 건물은 하회마을의 고택이라고 해도 될 고급 주거공간입니다. 실제 봉정사에는 퇴계 이황[08]을 비롯한 안동의 유명 선비들이 방문하였는데, 하룻밤 묵어갈 수 있도록 해놓은 일종의 템플스테이 건물 아니었을까 생각됩니다. 요사 밖으로 달린 툇마루가 무척이나 멋스럽습니다.

- **06** 1575~1641. 15th King of Joseon.
  1575~1641. 조선 제15대 왕.

- **07** *Daeung-jeon* and *Geungnak-jeon* at Bongjeong-sa Temple in Andong are examples of *Geumdang*. This name refers to a Dharma hall that enshrines the main Buddha statue. It is said that Buddha emits a golden (*geum*) light from his body.
  한 사찰에서 모시는 본존 불상을 모신 법당을 이르는 말. 안동 봉정사 대웅전과 극락전을 금당이라 할 수 있다.

- **08** 1501~1570. A scholar and civil official of the mid-Joseon period. He is depicted on Korea's 1,000 won bill.
  1501~1570. 조선 중기의 학자이자 문신(文臣)으로 일천원권 지폐의 도안에 새겨진 인물.

Yeongsan-am Hermitage, the Third Area

Yeongsan-am, a hermitage of Bongjeong-sa Temple, is a secluded world with a unique air of tranquility, despite being located directly beside the temple. At its entrance is *Uhwa-ru* Pavilion, which is just as splendid as *Manse-ru* Pavilion but smaller. If one passes through the hidden entrance below it, a little garden comes into view. It forms a small universe of magnificent old pine trees and flower bushes. Sitting on the old wooden floor of *Uhwa-ru* Pavilion and enjoying the sounds of nature banishes thousands of years of stored up troubles from one's mind. *Eungjin-jeon*, a central hall of the hermitage, is located in one corner of the grounds. It enshrines a statue of Sakyamuni Buddha and sixteen arhats. Its three Buddha statues are overwhelmingly large compared to the size of the hall, seeming to fill the entire hall. Another attraction of *Eungjin-jeon* is the wall full of folk murals. Paintings of tigers, cranes, and dragons are also painted on the outer walls of the hall, making it literally a small exhibition of folk paintings.

Although small in size, the hermitage is relaxed and tranquil, and is where monks can take a break from the intense battle within themselves to attain Nirvana.

Yeongsan–am Hermitage, Andong
안동 영산암

제3의 영역, 영산암

봉정사의 암자인 영산암은 바로 옆에 붙어 있음에도 독특한 적막감이 휘감는 별개의 세계입니다. 입구에는 누각인 우화루가 펼쳐져 있는데, 규모는 작아도 만세루에 버금가는 멋진 건축물입니다. 그 아래의 비밀스런 입구를 지나면 아담한 정원이 나옵니다. 우람한 고송과 꽃나무가 어우러진 작은 우주이지요. 고풍스런 마루가 깔린 우화루에 올라 이 안에서 계절이 흐르는 소리를 듣고 있으면 그야말로 천년 묵은 근심이 다 사라지는 것 같은 기분이 듭니다. 영산암 안쪽 한켠에는 주불전인

응진전이 자리 잡고 있습니다. 응진전은 석가모니불과 16나한을 모신 곳인데, 전각의 크기에 비해 본존인 삼존상의 크기가 압도적으로 커서 전각 안이 꽉 찬 느낌입니다. 응진전의 또 다른 매력은 그 안을 가득 채우고 있는 민화풍의 벽화들입니다. 건물 바깥벽에도 호랑이와 학, 용 등의 그림이 그려졌으니 그야말로 응진전은 작은 민화 전시관 같은 곳입니다. 비록 크지는 않아도 넉넉한 영산암은 스님들의 열반을 향한 치열한 자기 싸움에서 잠시 쉬어가는 곳이라도 되는 것처럼 낭만이 가득합니다.

Another attraction of *Eungjin-jeon* is the wall full of folk murals.
응진전의 또 다른 매력은 민화풍의 벽화들이다.

If one passes through the hidden entrance below *Uhwa-ru* Pavilion, a little garden comes into view.
우화루 아래의 비밀스런 입구를 지나면 아담한 정원이 나온다.

Beopju-sa Temple

in Boeun County

보은

법주사

The Layout of Beopju-sa Temple
법주사 가람 배치도

1	*Geumgang-mun* 금강문	7	*Cheonwang-mun* 천왕문	14	Stone Standing Bodhisattva 희견보살상
2	Iron Pot 철솥	8	*Palsang-jeon* 팔상전	15	*Jinyeong-gak* 진영각
3	Stone Lotus Basin 석련지	9	*Beomjong-gak* 범종각	16	Four Heavenly Guardians Stone Lantern 사천왕석등
4	Rock-Carved Seated Buddha Statue 마애여래의상	10	*Gunghyeon-dang* 궁현당	17	*Seonhuigungwondang* 선희궁원당
5	*Neungin-jeon* 능인전	11	*Yaksa-jeon* 약사전	18	*Daeungbo-jeon* 대웅보전
6	Colossal gilt-bronze statue of Maitreya Buddha 청동미륵대불	12	Twin-Lion Stone Lantern 쌍사자석등	19	*Myeongbu-jeon* 명부전
		13	*Wontongbo-jeon* 원통보전	20	*Samseong-gak* 삼성각

Where the Dharma Resides

법이 머무는 곳

Mt. Songni-san takes its name from the term "*songni*," which means "to detach from the secular world." Choe Chiwon,[01] who once visited the site, wrote in his poem:

"The Tao[02] does not shy away from people, But people shy away from the Tao. Mountains do not abandon people, But people abandon mountains."

In other words, it is not the mountains that abandoned the people and became distant from the secular world, but people abandoned the mountains, thus the mountain became more deep and remote. But, once you enter Beopju-sa, it is easy to forget you are in the mountains. The spaciousness and tremendous scale of the temple gives one the feeling of having entered a temple in the middle of a city.

During the Three Kingdoms period, major temples were built in cities. Even during the time of Sakyamuni Buddha, temples were not hidden in the mountains. They were not placed in the hearts of the cities either, yet they did not necessarily forsake the rest of the world. In fact, it was impractical for monastics to reside deep in the mountains because they depended strictly upon the patronage of the public as they did not own any personal property. Therefore, if they removed themselves from the public, they could not satisfy even their basic needs, especially food.

속리산의 '속리(俗離)'란 '세속에서 떨어지다'는 뜻이라고 합니다. 이곳을 찾은 최치원[01]이 지은 시에서 '도는 사람을 멀리하지 않으나 사람이 도를 멀리하고, 산은 사람을 떠나지 않으나 사람이 산을 떠나네(道不遠人 人遠道, 山非離俗 俗離山)'라고 하였는데, 이에 의하면 산이 깊어 세속을 떠난 것이 아니라, 사람이 떠나 깊은 산이 된 셈입니다. 그러나 막상 법주사에 들어서면 그곳이 산중이라는 사실을 잊게 됩니다. 넓은 공간에 광활하게 펼쳐진 법주사의 장쾌한 규모에 도심사찰에 온 것 같은 느낌이 들기 때문입니다.

원래 삼국시대의 주요 사찰들은 도심에 세워졌습니다. 석가모니 재세 시절에도 절이란 결코 깊은 산속에 숨어 있지 않았습니다. 그렇다고 도심 한가운데 있었던 것도 아니지만, 결코 세상을 버린, 즉 '속리'한 곳에 있지는 않았습니다. 사실 승가가 산속 깊은 곳에 들어간다는 것 자체가 불가능했습니다. 사유재산이 없던 스님들은 대중들의 공양에 절대적으로 의존했기 때문에 대중들과 너무 떨어져서는 가장 기본적인 경제생활, 즉 먹는 문제를 해결할 수 없었기 때문이지요.

●01   857-?. A renowned writer of Unified Silla.
      857-?. 통일신라시대의 명문장가.

●02   The Tao, a word signifying the "Way," "path,"
      or "doctrine" as in the philosophical system of
      Taoism that advocates attainment of simplicity and
      naturalness.

How Temples Came to Be in the Mountains

It is widely believed that temples were driven out of cities due to political persecution. In truth, however, temples began migrating to the mountains even before their political exclusion, which implies they had become autonomous and economically self-sufficient.

The legend of Great Master Sinmi is as follows: Master Sinmi, renowned at the beginning of the Joseon period, resided at Beopju-sa Temple. One day, a group of bandits stormed into the temple. Great Master Sinmi calmly opened the temple's storehouse and invited them to take all of the temple's wealth. Excited, the bandits grabbed everything and left the temple, but even after walking all night, they discovered at dawn that they had just been walking in circles within the compound. Realizing that they were captives of Great Master Sinmi's spiritual power, they begged for forgiveness, to which Master Sinmi responded, "Gazing into your eyes, I can tell that you are all virtuous people. From now on, go live virtuously." Hearing this, the bandits cried and repented. The essential teaching of the story is about Master Sinmi's enlightened power and compassion, but from another perspective, the legend suggests that Beopju-sa Temple had abundant resources gathered from the surrounding area and had gained great economic stability by storing goods.

Of course, temples did not move to the mountains just to gain economic self-sufficiency and practice asceticism based on this autonomy. One does not go to the mountains to separate themselves from the world. Rather, one goes to the mountains to embrace the world for what it is. In other words, in the mountains, people could readily understand and accept one another without regard to social class. For those who come together at a mountain temple, the only thing that seems to matter is their shared belief in Buddhism.

Beopju-sa
보은 법주사

사찰이 산에 들어간 이유

절이 산속으로 들어간 이유를 흔히 정치적으로 배척을 받아 도심에 머물 수 없게 되었기 때문이라고 합니다. 하지만 그 이전부터 절은 산으로 들어가고 있었습니다. 이러한 현상은 절이 자생적인 경제력을 갖추게 되었음을 의미합니다. 법주사에서 전해지는 신미 대사의 설화를 살펴보면 이렇습니다. 조선 초에 명성이 높았던 신미 대사께서 법주사에 주석하실 때 산적 떼가 쳐들어 왔는데, 대사는 태연히 절의 창고를 열어 모든 재화를 다 가져가도 좋다고 하셨습니다. 도둑들은 신이 나 재물을 있는 대로 싸 들고 절간을 나가 밤새 걸었는데 아침이 되어 보니 법주사 경내를 빙빙 돌고만 있더라는 것입니다. 이에 신미 대사의 도력에 걸려든 것을 알고 용서를 구하니 대사는 "너희들의 눈을 보니 모두 착한 사람들이다. 이제는 착하게 살라." 하셨고 이에 산적들은 모두 눈물을 흘리며 참회했다는 내용입니다.

이 설화의 핵심은 신미 대사의 도력과 자비심이지만, 한편으로는 법주사 인근에서 꽤 많은 생산이 있었고, 이를 비축해 상당한 경제력을 갖추고 있었음을 짐작할 수 있습니다.

물론 절이 산에 들어간 게 자급이 가능한 경제력을 바탕으로 홀로 청정한 수행을 하기 위해서만도 아닙니다. 산은 속세를 버리는 장소가 아니라 오히려 속세를 끌어안을 수 있는 장소입니다. 다시 말해 신분의 구분 없이 모두를 그저 있는 그대로 끌어안기에 가장 좋은 장소였던 것입니다. 그래서인지 산사를 찾으면 누구를 만나건 그저 다 같은 불자라는 시선 외에 다른 생각은 사라져 버리고 맙니다.

Beopju-sa Temple, Boeun
보은 법주사

Enshrining Maitreya: Mountain Temples that Resemble City Temples

At Beopju-sa, large structures like *Ilju-mun* Gate, *Cheonwang-mun* Gate, *Palsang-jeon* Hall and *Daeungbo-jeon* Hall are arranged in a linear fashion. This linear layout is common among city temples, including Hwangnyong-sa Temple in Gyeongju City and Jeongnim-sa Temple in Buyeo City. Mountain temples, on the other hand, enjoy greater liberty in their layouts to best suit the surrounding topography. Such topography-centered layouts were considered ideal in East Asian architecture, but were hard to achieve in actuality. Beopju-sa is the most faithful living relic of this ideal.

During the Unified Silla period, Precepts Master Jinpyo decided to construct a temple on a broad flat portion of land in the mountains. When he discovered an auspicious plant(called *Gilsangcho*) growing on Mt. Songni-san, he asked his disciple Yeongsim to erect a temple there, which became Gilsang-sa Temple, the original name of Beopju-sa Temple. Not surprisingly, a place like Geumsan-sa Temple in Gimje City, where Precepts Master Jinpyo took ordination and eventually resided, shares a similar architectural arrangement with Beopju-sa Temple.

At Geumsan-sa, *Daejeokgwang-jeon* Hall(Hall of Great Peace and Light), the *Bangdeung*[03] Ordination Platform and *Mireuk-jeon* Hall(Maitreya Hall) are laid out in the shape of "ㄱ." Comparably, at Beopju-sa Temple, *Daeungbo-jeon* Hall, *Palsang-jeon* Hall and a colossal gilt-bronze statue of Maitreya Buddha are laid out in the shape of "ㄴ."

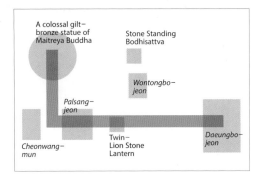

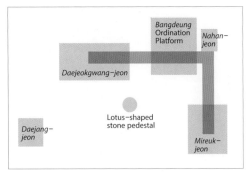

Beopju-sa's layout has an "ㄴ" shape(top image), while Geumsan-sa Temple's layout is in the shape of "ㄱ"(bottom image).
법주사의 'ㄴ'자형 가람 배치(위)와 금산사의 'ㄱ'자형 가람 배치(아래).

In other words, both temples have a pagoda at the center, and the buildings enshrining statues of Vairocana Buddha and Maitreya Buddha are situated at each end on an embankment line centered on the pagoda.

Moreover, Beopju-sa's *Palsang-jeon* Hall and Geumsan-sa's *Mireuk-jeon* Hall are both multi-story structures that render the two temples even more similar. Central to Precepts Master Jinpyo's philosophy was devotion to Maitreya Buddha. In fact, *Mireuk-jeon* Hall at Geumsan-sa and the colossal statue of Maitreya Buddha at Beopju-sa can be said to embody this ideology. Beopju-sa's huge gilt-bronze Maitreya statue clearly represents the temple's devotion to Maitreya Buddha. Originally, where the statue now stands, there used to be a *Yonghwabo-jeon* Hall enshrining Maitreya Buddha. Unfortunately, the statue once enshrined here, along with Beopju-sa's iron pole for hanging a large scroll painting, were requisitioned and perished during the late Joseon period. *Yonghwabo-jeon* Hall also eventually fell into ruin and was demolished. Then, in 1939, Kim Bokjin, a modern sculptor who created the giant statue of Maitreya Buddha at Geumsan-sa Temple, began building another colossal statue of Maitreya Buddha using concrete, but he passed away the following year, leaving it up to his disciples to complete. Regrettably, in the late 1980s, this statue developed cracks and was eventually torn down. The huge gilt-bronze statue of Maitreya Buddha now standing at Beopju-sa was constructed anew in the 1990s and was considered the largest in the world at that time.

Beopju-sa Temple enshrines yet another Maitreya Buddha. When one walks west from *Cheonwang-mun* Gate near the outer boundary of the temple, one will encounter a Rock-Carved Seated Buddha Statue(Treasure No. 216) from the Goryeo period engraved on a large cliff and posed as if sitting on a chair. The Buddha shown here is Maitreya Buddha. This is evidence further confirming that Beopju-sa Temple embodies Maitreya belief, which Precepts Master Jinpyo held in high esteem.

•03 *Bangdeung* means all those who receive ordination are equal.

도심사찰을 닮은 산중사찰, 미륵불을 모시다

법주사는 일주문부터 천왕문, 팔상전, 대웅보전에 이르기까지 대형 전각들이 일직선상에 위치하고 있습니다. 이는 경주 황룡사나 부여 정림사에서나 볼 수 있었던 도심사찰의 가람 배치입니다. 다른 산중사찰들은 산의 지형에 부합하게 비교적 자유로운 배치를 보이는 것과 대조적입니다. 이러한 배치는 동양의 건축에서는 항상 이상적인 배치이긴 했지만 실제 구현하기 힘들었습니다. 그럼에도 법주사는 그 이상을 가장 충실하게 반영한 살아 있는 화석과 같습니다.

산중에 이런 평탄하고 넓은 대지를 골라 절을 세우도록 한 것은 통일신라시대의 진표(眞表) 스님이었습니다. 스님은 속리산에 들어왔다가 길상초가 자라는 곳을 발견하고는 금산사로 돌아와 제자인 영심(永深) 스님에게 그 자리에 절을 세우라고 하셨는데, 그렇게 세워진 길상사가 법주사의 전신이었습니다. 그래서인지 진표 스님이 출가하고 주석했던 김제 금산사 가람 배치와 법주사 가람 배치는 서로 유사합니다.

금산사는 대적광전, 방등계단, 그리고 미륵전이 'ㄱ'자형으로, 법주사는 대웅보전, 팔상전, 그리고 청동미륵대불이 'ㄴ'자형으로 배치되어 있습니다. 즉 두 사원의 가람 배치는 모두 비로자나불을 모신 전각과 미륵불을 모신 전각이 탑을 중심으로 꺾인 축선 끝단에 위치하는 구조인 것입니다. 더욱이 법주사 팔상전과 금산사 미륵전이라는 고층 건물도 자리 잡고 있어 더욱 닮은 모습입니다. 더불어 진표 스님의 중심사상에는 미륵불이 자리 잡고 있었습니다. 그 때문에 금산사의 미륵전이나 법주사의 미륵대불은 모두 진표 스님의 미륵사상을 계승한 것으로 볼 수 있습니다.

법주사의 미륵사상을 가장 상징적으로 보여주는 것은 청동미륵대불입니다. 그런데 사실 그 자리는 미륵불을 모셨던 용화보전이 있었습니다. 아쉬운 것은 이곳에 모셔진 미륵대불은 조선 말 법주사 철당간과 함께 징발되어 사라졌고, 용화보전도 퇴락하여 헐렸다는 점입니다. 이후 금산사 미륵대불을 조성했던 근대조각가 김복진 선생에 의해 1939년부터 콘크리트로 미륵대불 조성이 시작되었는데, 이듬해 선생이 작고하는 바람에 제자들에 의하여 완성되었습니다. 하지만 이 불상마저도 1980년대 말부터 콘크리트에 균열이 발생해 결국 철거되고 1990년대 지금의 청동미륵대불이 당시로서는 세계 최대 규모로 새롭게

Colossal gilt-bronze statue of Maitreya Buddha, Beopju-sa Temple
보은 법주사 청동미륵대불

조성되어 지금에 이릅니다.
그런데 법주사에는 또 한 분의 미륵불이
모셔져 있습니다. 천왕문에서 서쪽으로
조금 걸어 외곽 경계에 해당하는 곳에
자리한 거대한 바위로 발걸음을 옮기면
마치 의자에 앉아계신 것처럼 표현된

고려시대의 법주사 마애여래의좌상(보물
제216호)을 만날 수 있습니다. 이 부처님이
바로 미륵불입니다. 진표 스님이
중요시했던 미륵신앙을 법주사가 계승하고
있음을 여기서도 확인할 수 있습니다.

Rock-Carved Seated Buddha Statue, Beopju-sa Temple
보은 법주사 마애여래의좌상

Beopju-sa Temple: Colossal in its Entirety

The first things to catch one's eye when one reaches the temple entrance are the two fir trees in front of *Cheonwang-mun* Gate. Just as the two gingko trees in front of a Confucian academy represent Confucian teachings, the two fir trees at Beopju-sa reveal the presence of Buddha Dharma. Perhaps these fir trees could be considered the temple's true *Ilju-mun* Gate.

After Beopju-sa Temple was burned to the ground in the Jeongyu War,[04] Great Master Samyeong began reconstructing *Palsang-jeon* Hall in 1605, and Ven. Byeogam Gakseong completed it in 1626. *Cheonwang-mun* Gate at the entrance to the temple was rebuilt in 1624, and statues of the Four Heavenly Guardians, the largest surviving historical object from the Joseon period, are presumed to have been built at the same time. Made of clay, the statues stand six meters tall.

Palsang-jeon Hall

Past *Cheonwang-mun* Gate stands the largest wooden pagoda that currently exists

A Heavenly Guardian in *Cheonwang-mun*, Beopju-sa Temple
법주사 천왕문 천왕상

Cheonwang-mun, Beopju-sa Temple
보은 법주사 천왕문

today, named *Palsang-jeon* Hall(National Treasure No. 55). There are comparable structures, including *Mireuk-jeon* Hall at Geumsan-sa Temple and *Daeung-jeon* Hall at Ssangbong-sa Temple, but these are *Buljeon*(Buddha Halls) that enshrine images of Buddhas and Bodhisattvas. *Palsang-jeon* Hall, on the other hand, functions not only as a Buddha Hall enshrining a Buddha statue, but also as a pagoda enshrining Buddha's *sarira*. Aligned in a straight line in front of *Palsang-jeon* Hall is *Daeungbo-jeon* Hall. Together, they preserve the ancient tradition of "one pagoda with one main Buddha hall."[05]

During the Three Kingdoms period, Hwangnyong-sa Temple in Gyeongju and Mireuk-sa Temple in Iksan had a massive wooden pagoda. Also, through excavation, several wooden pagodas were found at sites like the Wangheung-sa Temple Site and Gunsu-ri Temple Site in Buyeo, Silsang-sa Temple in Namwon, and Kirim-sa Temple in Gyeongju. These wooden pagoda sites reveal that just as many wooden pagodas were built as stone ones. Most wooden pagodas, however, were destroyed in times of war. Beopju-sa Temple's *Palsang-jeon* Hall is in fact the only one that has been rebuilt.

Wooden pagodas require very specialized skills to construct. After the Imjin War, when nearly everything had to be reconstructed, the neo-Confucian Joseon government prioritized rebuilding Confucian schools over restoring temples. Reconstructing a building as unique and large as *Palsang-jeon* Hall was a particularly difficult task during those trying times. Nevertheless, Beopju-sa Temple's *Palsang-jeon* was reconstructed. It is presumed that Great Master Samyeong insisted on restoring at least one wooden pagoda to compensate for the countless pagodas destroyed in the war.[06]

The name *Palsang-jeon*(Hall of the Eight Great Events) derives from the fact that it enshrines a *Palsangdo*("Painting of the Eight Great Events" in the life of Sakyamuni Buddha). Inside a *Palsang-jeon* Hall are *Palsangdo* paintings hanging above columns that seem to reach to the sky. It allows one to learn about the life of Sakyamuni Buddha while performing *tapdori* or circumambulation.[07] *Palsang-jeon* are similar in concept to stupas found in India. These stupas are embossed with the life stories and teachings of Sakyamuni Buddha, along with other Buddhist art, around the outer circumference for devotees to appreciate as they circumambulate to pay homage. Korean Buddhism and Indian Buddhism, despite certain visible differences, have these basics in common.

모든 것이 거대한 법주사

사찰 초입에 들어 우리의 눈길을 먼저
끄는 것은 천왕문 앞에 선 거대한 전나무
두 그루입니다. 향교나 서원 입구에 선
은행나무 두 그루가 공자의 가르침을
상징하듯 법주사는 전나무 두 그루로
이곳이 불법(佛法)이 머무는 곳임을
드러내고 있습니다. 어쩌면 이 전나무가
법주사의 진정한 일주문인지도 모릅니다.
법주사는 정유재란[04]으로 불탄 이후
1605년 사명 대사께서 팔상전을
재건하였고, 벽암 각성 스님이 이어받아
1626년까지 중창되었습니다. 사찰 초입의
천왕문은 1624년 다시 세워진 것으로서
이때 같이 조성된 것으로 추정되는
사천왕상은 현존하는 조선시대 것 중 최대
규모입니다. 흙으로 빚어 만든 천왕상은 그
높이가 6미터에 달합니다.

팔상전

천왕문을 지나면 현존하는 최대 규모의
목탑이 눈에 들어옵니다. 바로 법주사
팔상전(국보 제55호)입니다. 이와 유사한
구조로 금산사의 미륵전과 쌍봉사의
대웅전이 있지만 이는 불상을 봉안한
불전인 반면, 팔상전은 불전의 기능과
함께 부처님 사리를 봉안한 불탑의
기능도 했습니다. 팔상전과 일직선으로

배치된 대웅보전과 더불어 말하자면 '1탑
1금당'[05]의 오랜 전통을 고수하고 있는
셈입니다.
우리나라에는 삼국시대에 경주 황룡사나
익산 미륵사에 거대한 목탑이 세워져
있었습니다. 그리고 발굴을 통해 부여
왕흥사지와 군수리사지, 남원 실상사,
경주 기림사 등 수많은 목탑지가
확인되어 석탑뿐만 아니라 목탑 역시
많이 세워졌음을 알 수 있게 되었습니다.
그러나 목탑은 대부분 전란을 겪으며
사라졌습니다. 다시금 중창된 목탑은
사실상 이 팔상전이 유일합니다.
목탑은 건축적으로 매우 까다로운 기술이
필요합니다. 특히나 왜란 이후 거의 모든
것이 새로 지어지던 상황에서 성리학의
나라 조선에서는 사찰보다도 향교 등의
복구가 더 시급했습니다. 팔상전처럼
독특하고 거대한 건축을 복원하는 일은
이런 급박한 상황에 사실상 어려운
일이었습니다. 그럼에도 법주사의
팔상전은 복구되었습니다. 아마도 사명
대사가 전란 중 사라져 버린 많은 목탑들을
대신해 최소한 이것 하나만이라도 반드시
복원되어야 한다고 믿고 이 일을 강력하게
추진했던 것이 아니었을까 생각됩니다.[06]
'팔상전(捌相殿)'이란 명칭은 그 안에

The *Palsangdo* painting and the 1,000 Buddha statues are enclosed in *Palsang-jeon* Hall with its exquisite structural beauty
구조적인 아름다움이 돋보이는 팔상전 내부에 봉안된 팔상도와 천불상

석가모니의 일생을 여덟 장면으로 압축해 그린 '팔상도(八相圖)'를 봉안했기 때문에 지어졌습니다. 안에 들어가 보면 하늘을 찌를 듯 솟은 기둥들 위로 팔상도가 걸려 있지요. 안에서 탑돌이[07]를 하며 석가모니불의 일생을 읽을 수 있도록 배려한 것은 인도에서도 둥그런 불탑인 스투파 주위를 돌 때 볼 수 있도록 탑 둘레에 불전부조를 새겨 장엄한 것과 서로 통하는 방식입니다. 이처럼 눈에 보이는 형태는 달라도 한국불교와 인도불교의 기본 구조는 크게 다르지 않습니다.

[04] Japanese invasion which broke out after the Imjin War negotiations fell through.
임진왜란 중 교섭이 결렬되어 일어난 왜란.

[05] Traditional temple layout where a stone pagoda enshrining Buddha's *sarira* is positioned in front of the main hall that houses a Buddha statue.
부처님을 모신 주요 전각 앞에 부처님의 사리를 모신 석탑을 배치하는 사찰 가람 배치의 전통 양식.

[06] Salvaged from *Palsang-jeon* Hall, one *sarira* reliquary is currently on exhibit at the Dongguk University Museum. Its label indicates that the *Palsang-jeon* Hall was built thanks to Great Master Samyeong.
팔상전에서 수습된 사리장엄구는 현재 동국대 박물관으로 옮겨 전시되고 있는데, 사리외함의 명문은 팔상전이 1605년 사명 대사에 의해 세워진 것임을 기록하고 있다.

[07] *Tapdori* is based on a Buddhist ritual practiced in India where one circumambulates (walks around) a stupa or statue of Buddha in a clockwise direction as a means of showing respect.
인도에서 부처님 주변을 오른쪽으로 도는 '우요' 전통을 계승한 불교의식으로 이후 불상이나 불탑 주변을 도는 의식으로 발전했으며, 부처님에 대한 존경을 의미한다.

Daeungbo-jeon Hall

Perhaps a bit overshadowed by *Palsang-jeon* Hall and its fame, Beopju-sa's *Daeungbo-jeon* Hall(Treasure No. 915) is another notable Buddhist structure in Korea. *Gakhwang-jeon* Hall at Hwaeom-sa Temple, *Geungnakbo-jeon* Hall at Muryang-sa Temple and *Daeungbo-jeon* Hall at Magok-sa Temple are among the very rare two-story Buddhist halls remaining today.

Daeungbo-jeon was originally called "*Daeungdaegwangbo-jeon* Hall," a combination of "*Daeung-jeon* Hall"(which enshrines Sakyamuni Buddha) and "*Daegwangbo-jeon* Hall"(which enshrines Vairocana Buddha). In fact, *Daeungdaegwangbo-jeon* enshrined both Sakyamuni Buddha and Amitabha Buddha, with Vairocana Buddha in the center. These three Buddhas were sculpted in 1624 by Ven. Hyeonjin, a renowned sculptor in the 17th century who also created the Amitabha Buddha Triad in *Geungnak-jeon* Hall at Muryang-sa Temple in Buyeo.

Compared to Silla's Seokgur-am Grotto or Goryeo's captivating representations of the Buddha, Joseon's Buddha statues typically come across as crude, unbalanced, and too rigid. Understandably, worshipping idols was prohibited in neo-Confucian Joseon, which meant building statues that resembled the human form was frowned upon. In the same way that Confucian paintings focused on conveying spiritual messages over realistic images, Buddhist statues had to be as ideological and abstract as possible.

Furthermore, the Imjin War had brought countless deaths and injuries, so it did not make sense to create glorious and magnificent statues of Buddha with so many people suffering. But, a Buddha statue could not be depicted as wallowing in misery like sentient beings; what the people needed was a Buddha who could compassionately sympathize with the suffering of sentient beings and give them hope.

Ven. Hyeonjin's sculptures reflected and satisfied the needs of that era, confident yet withdrawn, rigid underneath bold and dynamic lines, and as fluid as water at first glance, but monotonous upon closer inspection. These contrasts were skillfully integrated into his Buddhist sculptures. Only upon understanding the loss and apprehension pervading the lives of the people in this period, can one begin to see the beauty in these statues.

Daeungbo-jeon at Beopju-sa, Boeun
보은 법주사 대웅보전

Vairocana Buddha Triad enshrined
in Beopju-sa Temple, Boeun(Treasure
No. 1360).
The statue of Vairocana is set at the
center flanked by Sakyamuni and
Amitabha Buddhas to his right and
left, respectively.
보은 법주사
소조비로자나삼불좌상(보물 제1360호).
비로자나불좌상을 중심으로
왼쪽은 석가모니불좌상, 오른쪽은
아비타불좌상이다.

대웅보전

법주사 팔상전의 유명세에 조금 가려졌지만 대웅보전(보물 제915호) 역시 우리나라 불전 건축을 대표합니다. 이러한 2층 불전은 구례 화엄사 각황전, 부여 무량사 극락전, 공주 마곡사 대웅보전 등 드물게 남아 있습니다.

대웅보전의 원래 명칭은 '대웅대광보전'이었습니다. 이는 석가모니불을 모시는 대웅전과 비로자나불을 모시는 대광보전이 합쳐진 이름으로 실제 그 안에는 비로자나불을 중심으로 석가모니불과 함께 아미타불을 모셨습니다. 이 세 부처님은 1624년에 조각승 현진 스님이 만든 것으로 스님은 1633년에 무량사 극락전의 아미타삼존불도 만들어 모신 17세기의 대표적인 조각승이었습니다.

일반적으로 조선시대의 불상은 신라의 석굴암이나 화려한 고려불화 속 부처님과 비교해 투박하고 균형도 맞지 않으며 경직된 느낌이라고 평가됩니다. 사실 조선은 성리학의 나라로서 우상 숭배를 금지했는데, 그런 조선에서 인간을 그대로 재현한 듯한 조각상 조성은 어려웠습니다. 마치 선비들의 그림도 사실성보다는 정신성을 전달하는 것이 중요했던 것처럼 불상도 최대한 관념적이고 추상적이어야 했습니다.

나아가 전쟁을 겪으면서 수많은 사람이 죽거나 다치고, 많은 것을 잃은 상황에서 부처님 혼자 어여쁜 모습으로 앉아계실 수는 없었습니다. 또 중생처럼 마냥 슬퍼하고 좌절할 수도 없었지요. 중생과 함께 슬퍼하되 희망을 주는 부처님이 필요했습니다.

현진 스님의 조각은 이런 시대적 요구를 반영한 작품입니다. 당당하지만 움츠러든 듯하고, 선이 굵고 역동적인 것 같지만 경직되었으며, 물 흐르듯 유려하지만 한편으로는 반복적인 틀에 갇혀 있습니다. 이런 이중성은 이 불상 안에 교묘히 공존하고 있습니다. 상실과 불안의 시대를 살았던 사람들의 시각을 고려하지 않으면 이 불상의 아름다움을 이해하기 어렵습니다.

Iron Pot of Beopju-sa Temple
보은 법주사 철솥

Another Famous Relic at Beopju-sa Temple

Thanks to their massive size, Beopju-sa's Iron Pot(Treasure No. 1413), flagpole support, and Stone Lotus Basin(National Treasure No. 64) make the temple seem like a land of giants. Moreover, stoneworks from Unified Silla, including the Twin-Lion Stone Lantern(National Treasure No. 5), Stone Standing Bodhisattva(Treasure No. 1417) and Four Heavenly Guardians Stone Lantern(Treasure No. 15), remind one that the temple has been standing since time immemorial.

The Twin-Lion Stone Lantern can be thought of as Beopju-sa Temple's mascot. Two powerful, muscular lions humbly holding up a stone lantern indicate how sacred the lantern is.

Some say the Stone Standing Bodhisattva is based on a tale of someone burning his arm to offer as a lamp to the Buddha, but others say it represents Kunlun Nu carrying an incense burner on this head as he leads people to Maitreya Buddha.

Not to be forgotten, another masterpiece is the Wooden Seated Bodhisattva Avalokitesvara(Treasure No. 1361) enshrined in *Wontongbo-jeon* Hall. Despite its unparalleled size when compared to other Joseon wooden Buddha statues, this statue exhibits details exquisite beyond description. Additionally, on either side of Bodhisattva Avalokitesvara are statues of Sudhana and the Dragon King, which are an interesting three-dimensional recreation of Naksan-sa Temple's Water-Moon Avalokitesvara painting that captures the moment where Great Master Uisang met the Bodhisattva. As we stare at Avalokitesvara's royal attire and divine clothes fluttering in the wind, it creates the illusion that Bodhisattva Avalokitesvara has instantly carried us to the ocean.

Stone Lotus Basin of Beopju-sa Temple
보은 법주사 석련지

법주사의 또 다른 대표 유물

법주사 철솥(보물 제1413호)과 당간지주,
석련지(국보 제64호) 등도 하나 같이
규모가 커서 마치 대인국에라도 온 것
같은 느낌이 들게 합니다. 여기에 더하여
쌍사자석등(국보 제5호)이나 희견보살상(보물
제1417호), 사천왕석등(보물 제15호)과 같은
통일신라시대의 석조물들은 이 절의 역사가
얼마나 유구한가를 보여주고 있습니다.
쌍사자석등은 법주사의 마스코트 같은
존재입니다. 탄탄한 근육을 가진 두 마리의
사자가 석등을 떠받들고 있는 모습은 이
등이 얼마나 존엄한 것인가를 설명합니다.

희견보살상은 자신의
팔을 태워 부처님께
등불을 공양했다는
설화를 바탕에 둔
것이지만, 이 상은
미륵불을 향해
나아가는 행렬을
인도하는 곤륜노가
향로를 머리에 이고 있는
모습을 나타낸 것이라는
해석도 있습니다.
여기에 덧붙여
빼놓지 말아야 할
걸작이 있으니 바로
원통보전에 봉안된
관음보살상(보물
제1361호)입니다.

이 상은 조선시대 목불상 가운데 유례가
드물게 큰 규모인데, 그럼에도 그 섬세함은
이루 말할 수 없습니다. 특히 관음보살상
양 옆에 있는 선재동자와 용왕의 상은
낙산사에서 의상 대사가 관음보살을 만난
장면을 그린 고려시대 수월관음도를
입체적으로 재현한 것이어서 더욱
흥미롭습니다. 그래서일까요? 바람에
나부끼는 관음보살의 관대와 천의 자락을
보고 있노라면 낙산사의 관음보살님이
우리를 순식간에 바닷가로 데려오신 것
같은 착각에 빠지게 됩니다.

Twin-Lion Stone Lantern of Beopju-sa Temple
보은 법주사 쌍사자석등

Stone Standing Bodhisattva of Beopju-sa Temple
보은 법주사 희견보살상

Wooden Seated Bodhisattva Avalokitesvara in *Wontongbo-jeon*, Beopju-sa
보은 법주사 원통보전 목조관음보살좌상

Vestiges of Great Monks at Beopju-sa Temple

There are three important pagodas at Beopju-sa. One is Sakyamuni Buddha's Sarira Pagoda, which stands behind *Neungin-jeon* Hall where King Gongmin of late Goryeo is said to have enshrined Sakyamuni Buddha's *sarira* from Tongdo-sa Temple. The other two are the stupas of Buddhist Monk Suam(Treasure No. 1416)[08] and Stupa of Buddhist Monk Hakjo(Treasure No. 1418), which is located at Bokcheon-am Hermitage farther up from Beopju-sa Temple. Great Master Sinmi, who played a crucial role in the creation of Korea's Hangeul alphabet, stayed at Bokcheon-am. In that sense, the hermitage can be considered the place of Hangeul's birth and development.

Mature pine trees encircle the two Sangha pagodas found on the mountains behind Bokcheon-am Hermitage, where it almost appears as if the trees have come to listen to the Buddhist master's discourse. On the road to Bokcheon-am Hermitage is the place where King Sejo[09] stopped to bathe when he came to meet Great Master Sinmi. The surrounding scenery is strikingly beautiful, and it is highly recommended to hike along this path.

Stupa of Buddhist Monk Suam at Bokcheon-am Hermitage of Beopjusa Temple, Boeun
보은 법주사 복천암 수암화상탑

법주사 고승들의 흔적

법주사에는 중요한 사리탑이 세 구가
있는데, 하나는 고려 말 공민왕이 통도사의
진신사리 1과를 옮겨 봉안했다는
능인전 뒤편의 세존사리탑이고, 다른 두
탑은 법주사에서 더 올라가 자리 잡은
복천암의 수암화상탑(보물 제1416호)[08]과
학조화상탑(보물 제1418호)입니다. 신미
대사는 한글 창제에도 중요한 역할을 했던
것으로 알려져 있습니다. 복천암은 그런
신미 대사께서 머무셨던 절이니 한글
창제와 발전의 산실이라 할만합니다.
복천암 뒤편 산중에 모셔진 두 분의 승탑
주변을 오래된 소나무들이 둘러서듯 자라고
있습니다. 마치 스님의 설법을 듣기 위해
모인 것 같습니다. 복천암 가는 길에는 신미
대사를 만나러 왔던 세조[09]가 목욕했다는
목욕소를 지나게 되는데 그 풍광도 매우
아름답습니다. 꼭 한 번 걸어 보시길
추천드립니다.

Stupa of Buddhist Monk Hakjo at Bokcheonam
Hermitage of Beopjusa Temple, Boeun
보은 법주사 복천암 학조화상탑

[08] This stupa enshrines the *sarira* of Great Master
Sinmi.
이 승탑은 신미 대사의 것이다.

[09] 1417-1468. 7th King of Joseon.
1417-1468. 조선 제7대 왕.

Magok-sa Temple

in Gongju City

The Layout of Magok-sa Temple
마곡사 가람 배치도

1	*Haetal-mun* 해탈문	**6**	*Myeongbu-jeon* 명부전	**11**	*Simgeom-dang* 심검당
2	*Heungseong-ru* 흥성루	**7**	*Cheonwang-mun* 천왕문	**12**	*Daegwangbo-jeon* 대광보전
3	*Suseonsa* 수선사	**8**	*Eungjin-jeon* 응진전	**13**	*Josa-jeon* 조사전
4	*Yeongsan-jeon* 영산전	**9**	Five-story Stone Pagoda 오층석탑	**14**	*Daeungbo-jeon* 대웅보전
5	*Maehwa-dang* 매화당	**10**	*Jong-gak* 종각		

Temple of Perfect Interfusion and Art

원융과 예술의 산사

There are two legends regarding Magok-sa Temple, which was established at the foot of Mt. Taehwa-san in Gongju, Chungcheongnam-do Province. The first legend states that it was founded by Great Master Jajang of Silla in the 41st year of the reign of Baekje's King Mu(640).[01] The fact that a temple in Baekje was established by a preeminent monk from Silla can be interpreted as evidence of cultural exchanges between the Three Kingdoms, regardless of military and political tensions.

The other legend holds that Master Muyeom[02] of Silla was the founder of the temple. Master Muyeom returned from Tang China after being taught by *Seon* Master Magok Bocheol. *Magok-sa Sajeokiban*, written in 1851, states that the temple was named Magok-sa because "the crowd that gathered for the Dharma talk of Master Bocheol were packed together like jute(*ma*, tight knit hemp fiber)." It is also said that Master Muyeom named the temple Magok-sa in honor of *Seon* Master Magok Bocheol.

According to records, Magok-sa Temple was later rebuilt by National Preceptor Bojo Jinul[03] who sought to unify the *Seon* School(a meditation-oriented school) and *Gyo* School(a doctrine-oriented school).

The appearance of Preceptor Jajang of the *Avatamsaka Sutra* School, Ven. Muyeom of the *Seon* School, and Ven. Jinul who pursued the integration of the *Seon* and *Gyo* Schools, in the establishment and reconstruction of Magok-sa Temple reflects the diversity of thought which served as the foundation of the temple. In fact, Magok-sa Temple enshrines Vairocana Buddha, the main Buddha of the *Avatamsaka Sutra* School, and Sakyamuni Buddha, whom the *Seon* School regarded as its foundational master. It also has a *Yeongsan-jeon* Hall, which symbolizes the doctrine of the *Lotus Sutra*[04] that Ven. Jinul attempted to incorporate. Consequently, examining how the temple harmonized and perfectly infused these three schools of thought is the first step to understanding Magok-sa Temple.

충청남도 공주 태화산 기슭 마곡사의 창건에 대해서는 두 가지 설이 있습니다. 첫 번째 설은 백제 무왕[01] 41년(640) 신라의 자장 스님이 창건했다는 설입니다. 백제의 사찰을 신라의 고승이 창건했다는 것은 아마도 정치·군사적 갈등과는 무관한 삼국 간 문화 교류 흔적으로서도 볼 수 있겠습니다.

다른 한 가지 설은 신라 무염 스님[02] 창건설입니다. 무염 스님은 당나라에서 마곡 보철 선사에게 가르침을 받고 돌아왔습니다. 1851년에 쓰인 「마곡사사적입안(麻谷寺事蹟立案)」에는 "보철 화상의 설법을 들으러 모인 사람이 마(麻)처럼 촘촘히 많았다."고 해서 마곡사란 이름을 얻게 되었다는 기록이 보입니다. 또 무염 스님은 마곡 보철 선사를 기려 절 이름을 마곡사로 했다고도 합니다.

한편 마곡사는 선종과 교종(敎宗)의 통합(定慧雙修)을 추구한 보조국사 지눌 스님[03]에 의해 중창되었다고 전합니다. 이처럼 마곡사의 창건, 중창과 관련해 화엄종의 자장 스님, 선종(禪宗)의 무염 스님, 그리고 선·교 통합을 추구했던 지눌 스님이 등장하는 만큼 다양한 사상이 바탕이 되었음을 짐작할 수 있습니다. 실제로 마곡사엔 화엄종의 본존인 비로자나불과 선종에서 근원적 스승으로 모시는 석가모니불이 모셔져 있으며, 지눌 스님이 겸하고자 했던 법화사상[04]의 상징인 영산전이 자리하고 있습니다. 이렇듯 세 종파가 한 사찰 안에서 어떻게 조화를 이루며 원융의 공간이 되었는지를 살펴보는 것이 마곡사를 이해하는 첫걸음입니다.

- 01   ?-641. 30th King of Baekje.
        ?-641. 백제 제30대 왕.

- 02   801-888.

- 03   1158-1210. A monk of the Goryeo period.
        1158-1210. 고려시대의 승려.

- 04   A Buddhist doctrine that was developed based on the *Lotus Sutra*.
        『법화경』을 근본으로 삼아 발전된 불교사상의 하나.

A Temple Nestled in an Auspicious Site

According to the geomantic rules of Feng Shui, Magok-sa Temple is situated in a very auspicious location. Nam Sago, a scholar of mid-Joseon, asserted the "Theory of *Sipseungji*" while identifying ten locations to take shelter in during wars or natural disasters. According to his theory, "the two streams of Yugu and Magok in Gongju can save all people," and Magok-sa Temple sits at the confluence of these two streams. Every visitor can intuitively sense they have entered a very auspicious site the moment they step into the temple. While most temples are located near a water source for obvious reasons, such as to support livelihood of monks and nuns, at Magok-sa Temple, the water flows through the temple complex. Similar to Tongdo-sa Temple, Magok-sa Temple is laid out in three general areas. However, unlike the orderly structure of Tongdo-sa Temple, these three areas seem to be randomly arranged, and the overall feeling is open and free. Although these areas seem detached from each other with no impression of a purposeful connection, they are somehow harmonious. In this way, while the individuality of each area is respected, the overall order is well balanced and harmonized. Such overall order is a model for the ideal relationship between modern society and the individual.

길지에 자리한 산사

마곡사가 자리한 곳은 풍수지리적으로 대단한 길지(吉地)라고 합니다. 조선 중기 학자인 남사고는 난리를 피할 수 있는 열 곳을 가려 '십승지론'을 주장했는데, 그중 "공주의 유구·마곡의 두 냇가는 만인의 목숨을 살릴 곳"이라 하였습니다. 이 유구천과 마곡천이 만나는 사이에 마곡사가 있습니다. 이곳이 명당임은 사찰에 들어서는 순간 누구나 느낄 수 있습니다. 대부분의 산사는 스님들의 생활을 위해 물을 끼고 있을 수밖에 없는데, 마곡사는 물이 아예 절 가운데를 관통합니다. 마곡사도 통도사처럼 세 개의 원으로 구성되어 있습니다. 그러나 배치 방식은 질서 있는 통도사와는 달리 각 원이 아무렇게나 놓인 것처럼 자유롭고 느슨합니다. 서로에게는 무심하며 굳이 통합하려는 의지도 보이지 않지만 조화롭습니다. 이처럼 각각의 개성이 존중되는 가운데 전체라는 질서가 유지되는 모습은 현대사회와 개인의 관계에 있어 가장 이상적인 모델이라 생각됩니다.

Magok-sa Temple, Gongju
공주 마곡사

The *Daegwangbo-jeon* Area

Many of Magok-sa's buildings were destroyed during the Japanese invasion of Korea but were later rebuilt by Master Gaksun in 1651. The temple's central hall, *Daegwangbo-jeon*(Treasure No. 802), was burnt down a second time in 1782 but was restored in 1813. It is a large hall measuring five *kan*s across the front and three *kan*s deep. It is topped with a hip-and-gable roof, and therefore it is often compared to *Muryangsu-jeon* Hall at Buseok-sa Temple which dates from the Goryeo period. However, Magok-sa's *Daegwangbo-jeon* Hall was built in the *dapo*-style that allows for more interior space for Buddhist services by eliminating a few columns that support the main crossbeams. At the same time, it radiates a natural beauty by using naturally curved tree trunks as columns at the front and rear sides, and four corners of the building. This architectural style is considered characteristic of Joseon Buddha halls.

Daeungbo-jeon(upper hall) and *Dagwangbo-jeon*(lower hall), Magok-sa Temple
공주 마곡사 대웅보전(위)과 대광보전(아래)

The Buddha enshrined here faces east like the Buddha in Buseok-sa's *Muryangsu-jeon* Hall. However, the Buddha at Magok-sa Temple is Vairocana Buddha forming the wisdom mudra of Vairocana(*Jigweonin*). If Buseok-sa Temple represents the Avatamsaka thought of early Unified Silla, Magok-sa Temple represents the Avatamsaka thought that was intertwined with *Seon* Buddhism in late Unified Silla. The age of this Buddha is unclear, but it has characteristics of Buddha statues from late Goryeo to the early Joseon period. Further research is required.

The sacred figures in the Buddhist painting hanging behind the main Buddha statue seem as if they emanate from the main Vairocana Buddha and spread across the entire Dharma Hall. This Buddhist painting, which dates back to the 12th year of King Jeongjo's reign(1788),[05] depicts Sakyamuni Buddha giving a sermon on the peak of Mt. Yeongchuk-san. Although Magok-sa's architecture, this painting, and the statue were all created during different time periods, the elements harmonize as though they were meant to be together. The Buddhist painting hanging on the back of the wall behind the main Buddha statue is a five meter tall scroll painting of Bodhisattva Avalokitesvara of Great Compassion in a white robe, known as *Baegeuigwaneumdo*. It is an important painting as it confirms Magok-sa's history of seeking enlightenment and belief in Avalokitesvara. The painting also depicts a young Sudhana praying to the Bodhisattva of Great Compassion of the Water-Moon. It depicts a scene from the *Gandavyuha*(chapter titled *Entrance into the Dharma Realm*) from the *Flower Ornament Sutra*. It is a scene where a young seeker of the truth(Sudhana), who visited 53 great enlightened masters for instruction, meets Bodhisattva Avalokitesvara on Mt. Potalaka on his 28th encounter.

Seated Vairocana Buddha in *Daegwangbo-jeon*, Magok-sa Temple
공주 마곡사 대광보전 비로자나불상

The inside of *Daegwangbo-jeon* Hall, Magok-sa
대광보전 내부

대광보전 영역

마곡사 전각들은 임진왜란 때 거의
대부분 소실되었다가 1651년에 각순
스님에 의해 중건되었는데, 중심 전각인
대광보전(보물 제802호)은 1782년에 다시금
불에 타 1813년에 또다시 지어졌습니다.
정면 5칸, 측면 3칸의 대규모 불전이면서
팔작지붕을 얹어 고려시대 건축인 부석사
무량수전과 비교됩니다. 하지만 마곡사
대광보전은 다포 구성의 전각으로서 내부에
대들보를 받치는 높은 기둥 일부를 생략해
예불 공간을 보다 넓게 확보합니다. 한편
전각의 네 모퉁이와 측·후면에는 자연
상태의 구부러진 나무를 그대로 기둥으로
사용하여 자연미를 살렸습니다. 이러한
방식은 조선시대 건축의 특징으로 자리
잡았습니다.

여기에 봉안된 부처님은 부석사
무량수전의 부처님처럼 동쪽을 바라보고
계시지만, 이 부처님은 지권인(智拳印)의
비로자나불입니다. 아마도 부석사가
통일신라 초기의 화엄사상을 대변하고
있다면, 마곡사는 통일신라 후기에 선종과
결합된 화엄사상을 투영하고 있기 때문일
것입니다. 이 부처님의 제작연대는 정확치
않지만 고려 말, 조선 전기 불상 양식도
다소 남아 있어 앞으로 추가적인 연구가
필요합니다.

불상 뒤에 걸린 후불탱화는
그림 속 존상들이 마치 이 본존
비로자나불상으로부터 발산되어
법당을 가득 메우는 것처럼 보입니다.
이 불화는 정조[05] 12년(1788)에 그려진
것으로서 석가모니불의 영축산 설법 장면을
그린 것입니다. 이처럼 대광보전은 건축,
불화, 불상의 조성 연대가 각각 다릅니다.
그럼에도 본래 짝이었던 것처럼 잘
어울립니다.

한편 후불탱화가 걸려 있는 후벽의
뒷면에는 높이 5미터가 넘는 커다란
백의관음도가 그려져 있습니다.
관음 도량으로 소개되는 마곡사에서
관음신앙의 전통을 보여주는 의미 있는
작품입니다. 수월관음께 예불드리는
선재동자가 함께 그려졌는데, 이 장면은
『화엄경』「입법계품」에서 선재동자가
방문한 53명의 선지식 중 28번째인
포탈락가산의 관음보살을 만난 장면을
그린 것입니다.

●05 1752-1800. 22nd King of Joseon.
      1752-1800. 조선 제22대 왕.

Baegeuigwaneumdo in *Daegwangbo-jeon*, Magok-sa Temple
공주 마곡사 대광보전 백의관음도

Hidden Treasure of *Daegwangbo-jeon* Hall

There is another hidden treasure at *Daegwangbo-jeon* Hall. Old reed mats that lie under the floor mat seem to symbolize the prayers and hopes of the countless people who have visited *Daegwangbo-jeon* Hall.

One legend says that a paraplegic started weaving the reed mat for the Buddha as he prayed for 100 days for his legs to be healed. Weaving the reed mats may have been a way for him to focus on his prayers. Surprisingly, after weaving and praying for 100 days, the crippled man stood up as though he was not crippled and walked out of the temple. It is likely that he forgot what he was praying for while he focused on weaving. He also may have forgotten he was a paraplegic. Master Maju Doil once asserted that "the ordinary mind is the Way." For the paraplegic, weaving the mat was his own way of chanting a dharani.

Magok-sa's Five-story Stone Pagoda(Treasure No. 799), which stands in front of *Daegwangbo-jeon* Hall, is unique with its Tibetan-style, Buddhist pagoda-shaped gilt-bronze top. According to *Magok-sa Sajeokiban*, Preceptor Jajang established seven temples, but only the pagodas at Gaya-sa and Magok-sa Temples were decorated with gold on the third level and hung with wind chimes made of pure gold. The five-story stone pagoda we see today is not the original built by Preceptor Jajang, but it bears traces of the gold-ornamented pagoda he erected. The Tibetan Buddhist style present in the upper part of the pagoda tells us that the Tibetan pagoda style spread throughout Eurasia via the Mongol Empire, and Korea was greatly influenced by it during the Goryeo period.

Old reed mats are a hidden treasure of *Daegwangbo-jeon* Hall.
삿자리는 대광보전의 숨겨진 보물이다.

Magok-sa
공주 마곡사

대광보전에 숨겨진 보물

대광보전에는 숨겨진 보물이 또 있습니다. 바닥의 장판을 들어 보면 그 아래에 오래된 삿자리가 깔려 있습니다. 반들반들한 삿자리를 보면 대광보전에 와서 기도하고 갔던 수많은 사람들의 소망이 전부 여기에 배어 들어간 것 같습니다.

이 삿자리에는 오랜 전설도 전해옵니다. 옛날 앉은뱅이였던 사람이 대광보전에 와 다리를 낫게 해 달라고 백일기도를 하면서 부처님께 보시할 요량으로 삿자리를 짰다고 합니다. 아마 기도에 집중하기 위해 수행의 일환으로 그랬는지 모르겠습니다. 그런데 삿자리를 다 짜고 100일의 기한이 되니 그 앉은뱅이가 마치 아무런 일도 없었다는 듯 일어나 걸어 나갔다는 것입니다. 아마 그는 자신의 소원이 무엇이었는지도 잊은 채 삿자리에만 집중했을 것입니다.

그래서 자신이 앉은뱅이였다는 사실도 잊어버렸겠지요. 마조 도일 스님은 '평상심시도(平常心是道)'라 했는데, 앉은뱅이였던 그에게 삿자리 짜는 일은 곧 염불이요, 다라니였던 것입니다.

한편 대광보전 앞에 서 있는 마곡사 오층석탑(보물 제799호)은 맨 위에 티베트식 불탑 모양의 금동제 상륜부가 올라가 있어 특이합니다. 「마곡사사적입안」에서는 자장 스님이 세운 절이 일곱 곳인데, 그중 가야사와 마곡사 탑만 3층을 금으로 장식하고 순금 풍경을 달았다고 전합니다. 현재의 오층석탑은 자장 스님이 세운 탑은 아니지만 스님이 세웠다는 순금으로 장엄된 탑의 흔적으로 볼 수 있습니다. 탑 상륜부에서 볼 수 있는 것과 같은 티베트 불교 양식은 몽골제국을 통해 유라시아로 퍼져 나갔는데, 우리나라의 경우 고려시대에 많은 영향을 받았습니다.

The *Daeungbo-jeon* Hall Area

Daeungbo-jeon Hall is located behind *Daegwangbo-jeon* Hall, and its foundation is constructed on three layers.

Magok-sa's *Daeungbo-jeon* Hall(Treasure No. 801) is a two-story building with a hip-and-gable roof. It measures five *kan*s across the front and four *kan*s deep. The current hall was reconstructed in 1651(the 2nd year of King Hyojong's reign)[06] after being burned down during the Japanese invasion of Korea.

Many Buddhist halls, such as Magok-sa's *Daeungbo-jeon* Hall, were built as multi-storied buildings during the Joseon period; however, most of them were reduced to single stories during reconstruction in late Joseon. Hence, *Daeungbo-jeon* Hall is an exception as it remains as a two-story building. Although it is smaller than the two-story halls at Beopju-sa and Hwaeom-sa Temples, the composition of the components is meticulous, and wooden columns made from naturally curved tree trunks reflect the characteristics of the times.

Inside, all the columns normally found in front of the Buddha altar are left out, and the Buddha altar sits slightly set back from the center of the floor. In this way, *Daeungbo-jeon* Hall has a wide space that is exhilaratingly open to the ceiling of the second floor without pillars, and the sunlight enters through windows on the second floor, evenly filling the interior of the hall with light.

Three Buddhas – Amitabha Buddha, Sakyamuni Buddha, and Bhaisajyaguru Buddha(Medicine Buddha) from left respectively – are enshrined on the wide altar. Although the exact production dates of these statues are unknown, it

Three Honored Buddhas in *Daeungbo-jeon*, Magok-sa Temple
마곡사 대웅보전 삼세불상

is estimated that they were produced together around 1651 when *Daeungbo-jeon* was rebuilt. *Sajeokgi* states that Master Unhye, the abbot of Magok-sa Temple at the time, was assigned to be the head artisan because he was a master sculptor. As such, it is reasonable to believe that these statues of the Buddhas of the Three Worlds passed through the hands of Master Unhye.

These Joseon period Buddha statues have larger heads and hands than real people, and therefore, appear awkward. However, there is a reason for this. In Joseon, where Buddhism was repressed and Confucianism was propagated, building a large Buddha statue was prohibited. As a result, Buddha statues with large heads and hands could compensate for their smaller size, giving them a more commanding presence in the large hall.

It is said that the calligraphy on the current name plaque hanging on *Daeungbo-jeon* Hall was a collected characters of Kim Saeng,[07] a renowned calligrapher of Unified Silla. Comparing the calligraphy on the stele for Great Master Nanggong that features the calligraphy style said to be similar to Kim Saeng's, the winding calligraphy style on *Daeungbo-jeon*'s plaque looks similar at first glance, so it is understandable why some people believe it was written by him.

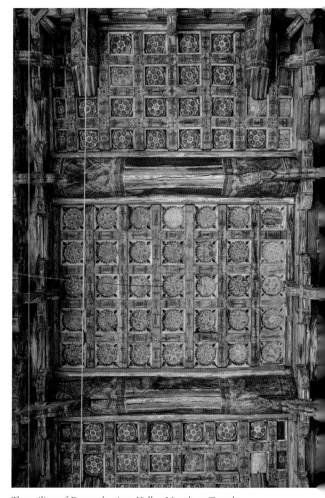

The ceiling of *Daeungbo-jeon* Hall at Magok-sa Temple
마곡사 대웅보전 천장

대웅보전 영역

대웅보전 영역은 대광보전 뒤편에 세 개의 단을 만들어 조성되었습니다.

마곡사 대웅보전(보물 제801호)은 정면 5칸, 측면 4칸의 평면에 팔작지붕을 지닌 2층 건축물입니다. 현재의 전각은 임진왜란 때 불탄 것을 효종^{•06} 2년(1651)에 중건한 것으로 전합니다.

마곡사 대웅보전처럼 조선시대에는 중층으로 세워진 불전이 많았지만 대부분 조선 후기에 중수되는 과정에서 단층으로 축소시킨 경우가 많습니다. 그런 가운데 대웅보전은 드문 경우로 2층 전각을 유지하고 있지요. 비록 규모는 법주사, 화엄사의 2층 전각보다 작지만 부재의 짜임새는 치밀하며, 자연적으로 구부러진 형태를 그대로 사용한 나무 기둥 등은 시대적 특징을 반영합니다.

내부에는 불단 앞 열에 있어야 할 기둥들을 모두 생략하고, 불단은 중앙에서 약간 뒤편으로 물러나게 설치했습니다. 이렇게 해서 대웅보전은 기둥 없이 그대로 2층 천장까지 뻥 뚫린 장쾌한 공간이 되었고, 2층의 창으로 햇살이 은은하게 들어와 법당 내부를 고루 비춥니다.

넓은 불단 위에는 향좌측부터 아미타불, 석가모니불, 약사여래불의 삼세불을 봉안하였습니다. 이 삼세불상의 정확한 제작연대는 밝혀지지 않았지만, 대웅보전이 중건된 1651년을 전후하여 함께 제작된 것으로 추정합니다. 그 당시 마곡사의 주지였던 운혜 스님은 유명한 조각 장인으로 「사적기」에 그가 편수를 맡았다는 기록이 있어 이 삼세불상 역시 운혜 스님의 손을 거쳤을 것으로 보기도 합니다.

이러한 조선시대 불상들은 실제 인체 비례보다 머리와 손을 크게 만들어 어색한 느낌이 들기도 합니다. 그러나 거기에는 나름의 이유가 있습니다.

억불숭유의 조선에서는 불상을 크게 만들 수 없었습니다. 그러다 보니 아담한 비례 대신 큰 머리와 손으로 예불자의 시선을 집중시킴으로써 작은 크기임에도 큰 법당 안에서 당당한 존재감을 부각시킬 수 있었던 것입니다.

한편 현재의 대웅보전 편액은 통일신라시대의 명필 김생^{•07}의 글씨를 집자하여 만든 것으로 전합니다. 김생의 진적(眞蹟)을 반영한 것으로 평가받는 낭공대사비의 서체와 비교해보면 '대웅보전' 현판의 구불구불한 필체가 언뜻 유사해 보여 왜 김생의 서체라고 했는지 짐작이 갑니다.

•06 1619-1659. 17th King of Joseon.
1619-1659. 조선 제17대 왕.

•07 711-?. A calligrapher of Unified Silla.
711-?. 통일신라시대의 서예가.

Completion of Magok-sa Temple's Five Buddhas

There are five Buddhas that were central to Buddhism during the Joseon period, and three of them are included in the Buddha's Trifold Body(*trikaya*): the Truth Body of Vairocana Buddha, the Enjoyment Body of Nosana Buddha, and the Emanation Body of Sakyamuni Buddha. In addition, the Buddhas of the Three Worlds are: Sakyamuni Buddha, Amitabha Buddha, and Bhaisajyaguru Buddha(Medicine Buddha). They are sometimes depicted in Buddhist paintings, such as in paintings of the Assemblies of the Five Buddhas at Chiljang-sa Temple in Anseong and at Buseok-sa Temple. This is the result of efforts to integrate the Trifold Body of the Buddha and the Three Buddhas of the Three Worlds to encompass every Buddha. The five Buddhas in the painting of Assemblies of Five Buddhas can also be found at Magok-sa Temple. First, the three Buddhas in *Daeungbo-jeon* Hall and Vairocana Buddha in *Daegwangbo-jeon* Hall make a total of four Buddhas. This is the same number of Buddhas as in the painting of Four Buddhas in the National Museum of Korea. However, although the name of the Buddha depicted in Magok-sa's *gwaebul* painting(Treasure No. 1260) is said to be Sakyamuni Buddha, it is actually Sambhogakaya, or Nosana Buddha. Therefore, if the *gwaebul* painting is spread out in front of *Daegwangbo-jeon*, it in effect completes the painting of the Assemblies of Five Buddhas. As an organic extension of the Five Buddhas, Magok-sa Temple is a space where everything is realized.

Furthermore, the four Buddhas are carved on four sides of the Five-story Stone Pagoda mentioned earlier. In addition, the sacred relics inside the pagoda symbolize Sakyamuni Buddha, so it can be said to represent the Five Buddhas. The southern and northern branches of Magok Stream meet near this pagoda. Also, the Five Buddhas are symbolized by the Five-story Stone Pagoda. Therefore, Magok-sa's pagoda and *gwaebul* painting are the connecting points for the infinite worlds of the Buddha that extend throughout the temple.

Hanging scroll painting of Buseoksa Temple, Yeongju (Five Buddhas) (Treasure No. 1562)
영주 부석사 오불회 괘불탱 (보물 제1562호)

Seated Amitabha Buddha in
Daeungbo-jeon
대웅보전 아미타불좌상

Seated Vairocana Buddha in
Daegwangbo-jeon
대광보전 비로자나불좌상

Seated Medicine Buddha in
Daeungbo-jeon
대웅보전 약사불좌상

Seated Sakyamuni Buddha in
Daeungbo-jeon
대웅보전 석가모니불좌상

Hanging Scroll Painting of
Magok-sa Temple
(Sakyamuni Buddha)
공주 마곡사 석가모니불 괘불탱

마곡사 다섯 부처님 도상의 완성

비로자나불을 중심으로 노사나불, 석가모니불의 삼신불(三身佛)과 석가모니불을 중심으로 아미타불, 약사불의 삼세불(三世佛)을 합쳐 조선시대 가장 핵심이 되었던 다섯 부처님을 5불이라 합니다. 이 다섯 부처님은 한 폭의 불화에 묘사되기도 하는데 안성 칠장사나 부석사의 오불회도가 그렇습니다. 삼신과 삼세를 통합하여 모든 부처님을 망라하고자 했던 노력의 결과입니다.

마곡사에도 오불회도와 같은 다섯 부처님의 도상이 나타납니다. 먼저 대웅보전의 삼세불과 대광보전의 비로자나불을 합하면 4불이 구성됩니다. 이는 국립중앙박물관 소장의 사불회도 도상과 같습니다.

그런데 마곡사 소장의 괘불탱(보물 제1260호)에 그려진 존상의 명칭은 석가모니불이지만, 실제 노사나불 도상을 하고 있어 대광보전 앞에 괘불탱을 펼치면 완전한 '오불회도'의 도상이 됩니다. 5불, 다섯 부처님이 유기적으로 확장되듯 마곡사에 모두 구현되는 셈입니다. 더욱이 앞서 설명한 오층석탑에도 4면불이 새겨져 있습니다. 여기에 더해 탑 안에 모셔진 사리는 석가모니불을 의미하므로 이 역시 5불의 표현이라 할 수 있습니다. 마곡천 남쪽과 북쪽 영역은 이 탑을 접점으로 만나고, 탑 안에 5불이 함축되어 있으니 괘불탱과 오층석탑은 마곡사 안에 중중무진 펼쳐지는 부처님 세계의 공간을 연결해 주는 접점이라 할 수 있습니다.

A Buddha carved on the side of the Five-story Stone Pagoda
마곡사 오층석탑 측면에 새겨진 부처님

Yeongsang-jeon Area

Yeongsan-jeon Hall(Treasure No. 800), formerly called *Cheonbul-jeon*, stands alone near the southern branch of Magok Stream. Its axial lines are also different from the other buildings. It is believed that the temple's buildings were positioned according to their roles: *Daegwangbo-jeon* Hall and *Daeungbo-jeon* Hall were for chanting prayers, and *Yeongsan-jeon* Hall was for cultivation of meditation practices. According to records, *Yeongsan-jeon* Hall was reconstructed in 1651, along with *Daeungbo-jeon* Hall, and was later repaired in 1842. It measures five *kans* across the front, is three *kans* deep, and is topped with a gable roof. However, the complex brackets more closely resemble a bracket wing structure that is inserted and interlocks with the upper part of the columns.

According to records, the name plaque for *Yeongsan-jeon* Hall was written by King Sejo. King Sejo, who ascended to the throne as a result of the *Gyeyujeongnan*[08] coup, came to Magok-sa Temple to persuade Kim Siseup,[09] who had criticized him and then secluded himself at the temple. However, Kim Siseup heard this and left the temple to avoid the king. Ultimately, King Sejo was unable to meet him and was disappointed, so he bestowed a handwritten signboard upon *Yeongsan-jeon* Hall, which was then under construction.

Yeongsan-jeon Hall, which symbolizes Mt. Yeongchuk-san, usually enshrines the Buddhas of the Three Times[10] that represent the past(Dipamkara Buddha), present(Sakyamuni Buddha), and future(Maitreya Buddha who is currently a Bodhisattva). In contrast, Magok-sa's *Yeongsan-jeon* Hall also enshrines seven Buddhas of the past[11] and statues of Arhats who were Buddha's enlightened disciples. The 1,000 Buddhas of the present kalpa are enshrined as well.

The seven Buddhas of the past are based on the concept that those who were recognized to have some spiritual achievement constantly manifest this in the world. Therefore, the concept of the seven Buddhas of the past is an expansion of the Buddhas of Three Times. The 1,000 Buddhas of the present kalpa are a visualization of Buddha's presence throughout the universe. If the seven past Buddhas symbolize Multiple Buddhas in terms of early Buddhism, the 1,000 Buddhas of the present kalpa represent Multiple Buddhas in terms of space in the context of Mahayana Buddhism. Therefore, *Yeongsan-jeon* Hall is an expression of the constant emergence of Buddhas in both time and space. Furthermore, it represents the possibility that all people living through all stages of their lives can achieve enlightenment.

The use of naturally curved tree trunks as the main crossbeams to support the ceiling is also significant. The curve of the stately crossbeams creates a dynamic atmosphere as if a dragon is flying overhead. As it would have been difficult to intentionally obtain several similarly curved beams, it can be assumed that the natural beauty of this look was in fact intended.

Perhaps *Yeongsan-jeon* Hall, which is a reproduction of the dharma talk depicted in the *Lotus Sutra*, represents the actual Mt. Yeongchuk-san that is seen as the secular world of conventional truth(*sokje*). On the other hand, *Daegwang-jeon* Hall and *Daeungbo-jeon* Hall across Magok Stream are intended to represent the transcendent world of ultimate truth(*Jinje*), which stretches from Mt. Sumi-san(Mt. Meru) to the Heaven of 33 Gods.

Yeongsan-jeon at Magok-sa Temple, Gongju
공주 마곡사 영산전

영산전 영역

과거에는 천불전(千佛殿)으로 불리던
영산전(보물 제800호)은 마곡천 건너 남쪽
구역에 별도로 위치해 있습니다. 또한
축선도 다릅니다. 기능적으로 대광보전과
대웅보전은 예불 공간, 영산전은 수행
공간으로 역할이 구분되었던 것으로
추정합니다.

영산전은 대웅보전과 함께 1651년에
중건되었고, 1842년에 중수된 기록이
있습니다. 정면 5칸, 측면 3칸의 주심포
맞배지붕 형식인데, 다만 공포가 기둥 머리
부분에 삽입되어 맞물린 익공식 공포에
가깝습니다.

영산전의 편액은 세조의 어필이라고
합니다. 계유정난[08]을 일으켜 왕위에
오른 세조는 자신을 비판하던 김시습[09]이
마곡사에 은둔하고 있다는 소식을 듣고
직접 그를 만나 설득하기 위해 마곡사로
왔다고 합니다. 그러나 소식을 들은
김시습은 세조를 피해 마곡사를 떠났고,
결국 만남이 이루어지지 못하자 세조는
아쉬운 마음에 당시 건축 중이던 영산전에
편액을 하사하고 떠났다는 사연입니다.

영축산을 뜻하는 영산전에는
일반적으로 과거(제화갈라보살),
현재(석가모니불), 미래(미륵보살)를 상징하는
수기삼존불[10]이 봉안되는데, 마곡사
영산전은 과거칠불[11]과 나한상을 함께

Inside of *Yeongsan-jeon*, Magok-sa Temple
마곡사 영산전 내부

봉안하였으며 그 뒤로는 현겁천불상을 봉안하였습니다.

과거칠불은 부처가 끊임없이 수기를 받아 세상에 출현한다는 사상을 바탕에 두고 있어서 수기삼존을 확장한 개념입니다. 현겁천불은 온 우주에 부처님이 두루 존재한다는 것을 시각화한 것입니다. 과거칠불이 초기불교에 있어서 시간적 의미의 다불(多佛)을 뜻한다면, 천불(千佛)은 대승불교에 있어서 공간적 의미의 다불입니다. 따라서 영산전은 시공간적으로 끊임없이 부처님이 출현한다는 개념을 표현한 것이며, 나아가 수많은 윤회전생을 살고 있는 우리 모두 그러한 부처의 경지에 오를 수 있는 가능성을 지니고 있음을 상징하는 것입니다.

천장을 받치는 대들보에 휘어진 나무를 그대로 사용한 것도 매우 인상적입니다. 모든 대들보들이 일률적으로 휘어진 모습은 마치 용이 일사분란하게 날아다니는 것 같아 역동적인 분위기를 자아냅니다. 이처럼 비슷하게 휘어진 대들보 여러 개를 일부러 구하기도 힘들었을 것이므로 이러한 자연스러운 모습은 실상 의도된 자연미였음을 짐작할 수 있습니다. 어쩌면 『법화경』 설법을 재현한 영산전은 실재하는 영축산, 즉 속세(俗諦)의 현실세계를 의미하고, 마곡천 건너 대광보전과 대웅보전은 수미산에서 33천으로 이어지는 진제(眞諦)의 초월적 세계를 의도한 것으로도 볼 수 있겠습니다.

• 08 A coup in 1453 led by Prince Suyang (later called King Sejo) to seize the throne.
1453년 수양대군(후에 세조)이 왕위를 빼앗기 위해 일으킨 사건.

• 09 1435-1493. Scholar of early Joseon.
1435-1493. 조선 전기 학자.

• 10 A prophecy in which the Buddha instructs a Buddhist practitioner on future enlightenment. The Buddhas of Three Times (授記三尊) are: Sakyamuni Buddha, Dipamkara Buddha (who foretold that the future enlightenment of Sakyamuni Buddha in the past life), and Maitreya Buddha (Sakyamuni Buddha foretold that the Maitreya will become a Buddha in the future).
부처가 수행자에게 미래의 깨달음에 대해 미리 지시하는 예언. 석가모니불과 석가모니불 전생에 미래의 깨달음을 예언한 연등불(제화갈라보살), 그리고 석가모니불이 미래에 부처가 될 것임을 예언한 미륵불(미륵보살)의 세 분을 수기삼존(授記三尊)이라 한다.

• 11 Buddhas who manifested themselves in past eons.
지난 세상에 출현했던 과거의 일곱 부처님.

Magok-sa Temple, a Buddhist Art University

Up until the modern period, Magok-sa Temple served as a *Hwaso*, a Buddhist school of arts and crafts. Three of these prestigious *Hwaso*s on the Korean Peninsula were: Heungguk-sa Temple in Namyangju(*Gyeongsanhwaso*), Yujeom-sa Temple on Mt. Geumgang-san(*Bukbanghwaso*), and Magok-sa Temple(*Nambanghwaso*).

Among the list of abbots who succeeded renowned Buddhist painter Ven. Woonhye, the name Ven. Sain stands out. He was revered for crafting Buddhist temple bells during the latter half of the 17th century. Additionally, *Gyeomsaibanwanmun* of Magok-sa Temple introduces a monk named Ven. Cheolhyeon who participated in renovating the temple. The text says he was "a monk who enjoyed life at the temple, practicing his talents in calligraphy and painting." He was also a renowned monk painter who left traces of his work in history.

Some traditions of the 17th century have continued into the modern period. The painting style of Ven. Geumho Yakyo, the predecessor of all monk painters today, has been passed down through Ven. Boeung Munseong, Ven. Geumyong Ilseop, and others. Today,

Ven. Seokjeong, who inherited this painting style, is considered a master Buddhist painter(*Bulhwajang*), in addition to being designated a living Intangible Cultural Property of Korea. At Magok-sa Temple, there is a *Bulmobirim* that pays tribute to Buddhist artists. At the *Bulmobirim*, a Buddhist ceremony called *Daryeje* is held every year, an event unique to Magok-sa Temple. According to the inscription on the stone monument of Ven. Hoeun Jeongyeon, "80 out of the 300 monks who resided at Magok-sa Temple at the end of the Joseon Dynasty were Buddhist painters." Therefore, Magok-sa Temple was indeed a Buddhist art school.

Why did this tradition of art prosper and develop at Magok-sa Temple? Magok-sa Temple has a legacy of monks who adhered to a variety of Buddhist thoughts, such as Master Jinul, who advocated *Jeonghye Ssangsu*(the equal cultivation of meditation and intellectual wisdom), and *Seon* monks like Masters Jajang, Muyeom, and Beomil. The teachings of these monks have influenced the evolution of Magok-sa Temple throughout the long pursuit of harmony and communication. Art is about dealing with communication,

which is fundamental to the very nature of
humans. It is no coincidence that the paths
of religion and art parallel one another.
Moreover, it is not by chance that amid
the harmonization of different modes of
thought at Magok-sa Temple, this temple
of *Bulmo*^{.12} was the result.

불교미술대학, 마곡사

근대기까지 마곡사는 화소(畵所), 즉 불교미술 공방학교의 역할을 해 왔습니다. 이러한 화소는 세 곳이 유명했는데 남양주 흥국사(경산화소)와 금강산의 유점사(북방화소), 그리고 이곳 마곡사(남방화소)였습니다.

화승이기도 했던 주지 운혜 스님을 이은 주지 명단에서 사인 스님도 눈에 띕니다. 17세기 후반 범종 제작으로 이름을 날렸던 스님입니다. 또한 마곡사의 「겸사입안완문(兼使立案完文)」에는 마곡사 중창에 참여한 스님 중에 철현 스님을 '글씨를 잘 쓰고, 그림을 잘 그려 절에서 노니던 스님'이라 소개했는데 이분 역시 화승으로서 행적을 남깁니다.

17세기의 전통은 근대로 이어졌습니다. 현재 활동하고 있는 화승들의 원조라 할 수 있는 금호 약효(錦湖若效) 스님의 화풍은 보응 문성(普應文性), 금용 일섭(金蓉日燮) 등의 스님으로 계승되었고, 현대에 와서는 국가중요무형문화재 불화장(佛畵匠)이었던 석정(石鼎) 스님으로 계승되었습니다.

마곡사에는 불교미술 제작 활동을 하던 분들을 기리는 불모비림(佛母碑林)이 있어 매년 다례재를 거행하고 있으니 마곡사만의 독특한 불교의식입니다. 호은 정연(湖隱定淵) 스님의 비에는 "조선 말 마곡사에 상주하던 300여 명의 스님 중 80여 명이 화승이었다."고 하니 마곡사는 그야말로 불교미술대학이었다고 해도 과언이 아닙니다.

왜 이런 예술이 마곡사에서 발전했을까요? 마곡사는 자장 스님으로부터 무염, 범일과 같은 선종 스님들, 정혜쌍수(定慧雙修)를 주장했던 지눌 스님 등에 이르기까지 다양한 사상을 지닌 스님들의 족적이 남아 있는 곳입니다. 그리고 이러한 가르침이 차곡차곡 쌓이면서 조화와 소통을 추구했습니다. 예술이란 인간 본연의 소통을 다루는 행위입니다. 종교가 지향하는 바와 예술이 지향하는 바는 이렇게 서로 닮았고, 여러 사상들이 마곡사에서 서로 융화되는 가운데 불모(佛母)*[12]의 사찰이 형성되었다는 것은 결코 우연이 아닐 것입니다.

• 12 A person who sculpts and paints Buddhist statues(*Bulsang*) and paintings(*Bulhwa*). 불상(佛像)이나 불화(佛畵)를 조각하고 그리는 사람.

Seonam-sa Temple

in Suncheon City

순천

선암사

The Layout of Seonam-sa Temple
선암사 가람 배치도

1	*Ilju-mun* 일주문	**10**	*Jijang-jeon* 지장전	**19**	Four stone cisterns 석조
2	*Cheukgan* 측간	**11**	*Daeung-jeon* 대웅전	**20**	*Dharma-jeon* 달마전
3	Seongbo Museum 성보박물관	**12**	*Muryangsu-jeon* 무량수전	**21**	*Jinyeong-dang* 진영당
4	*Beomjong-ru* 범종루	**13**	*Samseong-gak* 삼성각	**22**	*Mita-jeon* 미타전
5	*Beomjong-gak* 범종각	**14**	*Josa-jeon* 조사전	**23**	*Eungjin-dang* 응진당
6	*Simgeom-dang* 심검당	**15**	*Buljo-jeon* 불조전	**24**	*Sansin-gak* 산신각
7	*Manse-ru* 만세루	**16**	*Palsang-jeon* 팔상전	**25**	*Muu-jeon* 무우전
8	*Seolseon-dang* 설선당	**17**	*Wontong-jeon* 원통전	**26**	*Gakhwang-jeon* 각황전
9	Eastern and Western Three-story Stone Pagodas 동·서 삼층석탑	**18**	*Janggyeong-gak* 장경각		

The Continuing Legacy of Education and Scholarship in *Cheontae* Buddhism

천태 교학의 맥을 잇다

Mt. Jogye-san was named after the mountain where the Sixth Patriarch Huineng, the authentic lineage holder of Chan Buddhism in China, resided. National Preceptor Bojo Jinul gave it this name and then established Songgwang-sa Temple here. This temple has since become one of the three treasured temples of the Jogye Order which represent Korean *Seon* Buddhism. However, the monk who settled here first was National Preceptor Daegak Uicheon[01] who led the *Cheontae* School(Chin. Tiantai). Seonam-sa Temple was later reconstructed by Master Uicheon. It can be said that the two distinguished great Buddhist masters of Goryeo, Uicheon and Jinul respectively, built Seonam-sa Temple and Songgwang-sa Temple on the same mountain. However, the two masters never met, as Master Uicheon lived approximately 100 years before Master Jinul.

Despite the fact that they lived in different eras, the two monks – who had both visited Mt. Jogye-san either by coincidence or by necessity – held two ideas in common: Master Uicheon's philosophy of *Gyogwan Gyeomsu* and Master Jinul's philosophy of *Jeonghye Ssangsu*. Both of these philosophies were attempts to reconcile the *Gyo* School(doctrine-oriented school) with the *Seon* School(meditation-oriented school). The term *Gyogwan Gyeomsu* means "the concurrent cultivation of doctrinal study and meditation(Seon meditation)," and *Jeonghye Ssangsu* similarly means the "twofold balanced cultivation of meditation(the intuitive method of *Seon* Buddhism) and intellectual wisdom(the logic or reasoning of *Gyo* Buddhism)." Since these two masters, who sought to integrate these two Buddhist schools of thought, found their way to Mt. Jogye-san, this mountain can be considered a place full of the spirit of reconciliation and integration.

조계산(曹溪山). 선종의 절대적 존재인 6조 혜능 선사께서 머무시던 산의 이름을 따온 것입니다. 이렇게 이름을 짓고 이후 우리나라 선종을 대표하는 조계종의 삼보사찰 중 하나가 된 송광사를 창건한 것은 보조국사 지눌 스님이셨지만, 여기에 먼저 자리를 잡으신 분은 선종이 아닌 교종의 천태종을 이끄신 대각국사 의천 스님[01]이었습니다. 선암사는 바로 이 의천 스님이 중창하신 절입니다. 산 하나를 두고 고려시대의 쟁쟁한 고승인 의천과 지눌, 두 스님이 각각 선암사와 송광사를 키워내신 셈입니다. 그러나 두 분은 만난 적이 없습니다. 의천 스님이 지눌 스님보다 100년 정도 앞선 인물이기 때문입니다.

이렇게 시대를 달리했음에도 우연인지 필연인지 조계산을 찾은 이 두 스님은 공통된 생각을 가지고 계셨습니다. 바로 의천 스님의 '교관겸수(教觀兼修)'와 지눌 스님의 '정혜쌍수'입니다. 두 스님의 이러한 생각은 모두 당시 대립하던 교종과 선종을 어떻게 화합할 것인가에 대한 결론입니다. '교관겸수'란 '교학과 관법(선종의 참선)을 함께 수행한다'는 뜻이고, '정혜쌍수'도 '선정(선종의 직관)과 지혜(교종의 논리)를 함께 닦는다'는 뜻입니다. 이렇듯 대통합의 마인드를 가진 두 분이 이렇게 조계산이라는 하나의 산을 찾아 들어오셨으니 조계산은 회통과 통합의 넉넉한 공간인 셈입니다.

●01   1055~1101.

Master Uicheon and Seonam-sa Temple

As the fourth son of King Munjong,[02] Master Uicheon transitioned from being a prince to a monk. His father, King Munjong, was aware of problems within the Buddhist order of the time and sought its reformation. Moreover, he hoped that members of the monastic order would complete the reformation by themselves. It is possible that he may have actually wished for a leader from the royal family to emerge who would lead the monastic order. In response, Master Uicheon became a Buddhist monk at the age of 11 and learned mostly the doctrine of the Flower Ornament School(*Hwaeom* School) at Wontong-sa Temple in Gaegyeong. Also, after hearing of the fame of Dharma Master Jeongwon in Song China and exchanging letters with him, he expanded his knowledge of Buddhism.

However, Master Uicheon refused to simply follow the path predetermined by the royal family.

He wished to study in Song China. At the time, the Khitan people were emerging as the leading power in East Asia, surpassing the Song Dynasty. The Khitans continued to demand that Goryeo sever its relations with Song China and become an ally. However, although Master Uicheon stated he wanted to study in Song China,

the royal family could not allow him to do so. But in 1085, two years after King Munjong died and his older brother, King Seonjong,[03] was enthroned, Master Uicheon was able to travel to Song China disguised as a stowaway.

He also followed a different path than the religious order the royal family supported. At the time, the royal family primarily supported the Fa-Hsiang School(Characteristics of Phenomena School or Mind-Only School),[04] but Uicheon chose to learn the teachings of the Flower Ornament School. However, while studying in Song China, he chose the *Cheontae* School as his path. He is said to have pledged, in front of the pagoda of Zhiyi(the founder of Tiantai) that he would pursue the resurrection of Tiantai Buddhism in Goryeo, a decision not welcomed by any of the Buddhist schools in Goryeo.

After returning home, Master Uicheon was appointed abbot of Heungwang-sa Temple and led the publication of *Daejanggyeong*, the complete Buddhist canon that includes: Buddhist Scriptures(*Sutra*), Disciplines/Precepts(*Vinaya*), and Treatises(*Abhidharma*). This was the publication called *Sokjanggyeong* that followed the First Edition of the Tripitaka

Portrait of State Preceptor Daegak in Seonamsa Temple, Suncheon (Treasure No. 1044)
순천 선암사 대각국사 의천 진영 (보물 제1044호)

Koreana; *Sokjanggyeong* later became the basis of the *Palman Daejanggyeong*(Tripitaka Koreana). While he was actively engaged in practical matters such as the circulation of money, his mind was occupied by his plans to reform Buddhism, unite the Flower Ornament and Mind Only Schools, and integrate the *Gyo* School with the *Seon* School. In order to achieve his goals, a neutral location was required, so he chose Seonam-sa Temple on Mt. Jogye-san.

Seonam-sa Temple, Suncheon
순천 선암사

의천 스님과 선암사

의천 스님은 문종·[02]의 넷째 아들로서
왕자의 신분으로 스님이 되셨습니다. 의천
스님은 문종의 넷째 아들이라는 왕자의
신분으로 스님이 되셨습니다. 아버지 문종은
당시 불교 교단에 대한 문제의식을 가지고
개혁을 촉구했으며, 나아가 그 개혁을 승단
스스로 완성해 주길 원했습니다. 어쩌면
아예 왕실에서 승단을 이끌 지도자가 나오길
바랐을 것입니다. 이에 부응해 11세에
출가한 의천 스님은 개경 원통사에서
주로 화엄종을 배우셨고, 송나라의 정원
법사(淨源法師)의 명성을 듣고 편지로 질문을
주고받으며 불교의 폭을 넓혀갔습니다.
그러나 왕자 출신의 의천 스님은 왕실이
정한 길만 걷지는 않았습니다.
스님은 송나라에 유학을 떠나고자 했습니다.
당시는 동아시아 정세에서 거란이 송을
제치고 맹주로 떠오르고 있었습니다.
거란은 고려에게 계속해서 송과의 관계를
끊고 자신들과 통교할 곳을 요구해 왔지요.
그런데 의천 스님이 송나라로 유학을
가겠다고 하니 왕실에서는 허락할 수
없었습니다. 그래서 스님은 아버지인 문종이
승하하고 형인 선종·[03]이 즉위한 2년 뒤인
1085년이 돼서야 변장한 채 밀항하여
송나라로 건너갈 수 있었습니다.
또한 왕실이 추구하던 종파와는 다른 길로

가셨습니다. 당시 왕실은 법상종·[04]을 주로
지지하고 있었고, 자신이 처음 배우기
시작한 것은 화엄종이었습니다. 그러나
송나라 유학 동안 스님은 천태종을 자신의
길로 정했습니다. 스님은 천태종을 창시한
지자대사 지의 스님의 부도 앞에서 고려에
천태종을 부활시킬 것을 맹세했다고 합니다.
이러한 그의 행보는 어느 종파에서든
환영할만한 일이 아니었습니다.
귀국 후에는 흥왕사 주지에 임명되어 대장경
간행을 이끌었습니다. 이것이 초조대장경에
이은 속장경으로 팔만대장경의 기초가 된
사업이었습니다. 또한 화폐 유통을 추진하는
등 현실적인 문제에도 적극 참여하는 모습을
보였지만 속내는 불교의 개혁, 그리고
화엄종과 법상종의 융합, 교종과 선종의
통합을 위한 구상에 가득 차 있으셨습니다.
그러한 자신의 뜻을 펼치기 위해서는
독립적인 공간이 필요해 이곳 조계산
선암사를 선택하신 것입니다.

- •02 1019-1083. 11th King of Goryeo.
  1019-1083. 고려 제11대 왕.
- •03 1049-1094. 13th King of Goryeo.
  1049-1094. 고려 제13대 왕.
- •04 A religious school established during Unified Silla,
  which became one of the two largest Buddhist
  schools, the other being the *Hwaeom* School.
  통일신라시대에 성립된 종파로 고려시대 화엄종과
  함께 교종의 2대 종파가 되었다.

The Ponds of Seonam-sa Temple

The initial establishment of Seonam-sa Temple is known to have been completed by National Preceptor Doseon[05] at the end of the Unified Silla period. Perhaps that is why its name and location conform to the theory of Feng Shui. It is said that there are three famous boulders in the Honam region: Unam on Mt. Baekgye-san in Gwangyang, Seonam on Mt. Jogye-san in Suncheon, and Yongam on Mt. Wolchul-san in Yeongam. National Preceptor Doseon built Unam-sa, Seonam-sa, and Yongam-sa Temples at these three locations. In addition, legend says the boulder called Seonam is sacred and was bestowed by an immortal mountain hermit. That is why the beautiful stone arched bridge one crosses before entering Seonam-sa Temple is referred to as *Seungseon-gyo* Bridge(Treasure No.400); it is viewed as a bridge where an ordinary man can ascend to the realm of the gods. After crossing this bridge, one encounters *Gangseon-ru* Pavilion, which fulfills a role similar to *Ilju-mun* Gate, and means "a pavilion an immortal mountain hermit has descended to." In this way, by contrasting "ascending" with "descending," the point of contact becomes the boundary between the sacred and profane.

After passing *Gangseon-ru* Pavilion and walking toward *Ilju-mun* Gate, one encounters a pond called *Samindang*. This pond has a particularly unusual oval shape. Since many Korean traditional ponds have a square shape, it was speculated that these unique oval-shaped ponds were designed in the modern era. However, a similar oval shaped pond at Silsang-sa Temple in Namwon is known to date from the Goryeo period so there is an increased likelihood that the *Samindang* is also from the Goryeo period. Such ponds are referred to as "*dang*," meaning "embankment or levee." This suggests that *Samindang* was not merely ornamental, but was also possibly a water source to irrigate surrounding agricultural areas. Because the monks who lived here did not depend on support from the outside but developed and cultivated the hilly land around the temple to support themselves, it is assumed that such embankments served a practical purpose for the temple to achieve self-sufficiency. In particular, considering that several ponds are located close to *Samindang* and within the temple grounds, and considering that there are also tea fields in the area around Seonam-sa, we can presume that these ponds were used for other purposes beyond simple

Seungseon-gyo Bridge, Seonam-sa Temple, Suncheon
순천 선암사 승선교

Gangseon-ru Pavilion, Seonam-sa Temple, Suncheon
순천 선암사 강선루

ornamentation. Nevertheless, because an island was placed in the middle of these ponds to add to their picturesque beauty, just like *Samindang*, it certainly can be said to be the result of a delicate, artistic touch. On the way to *Ilju-mun* Gate are towering trees stretching up toward the sky, resembling a primeval forest. Thus, before passing through *Ilju-mun* Gate, the existence of the temple beyond the gate is not apparent. The small *Ilju-mun* Gate, which seems to be hiding the secrets of Seonam-sa Temple, features a gigantic roof. The temple contains neither statues of *Geumgang Yeoksa*(Vajrapani or vajra-warriors) nor images of *Sacheonwang*(Four Heavenly Guardians). Instead, its *Ilju-mun* Gate is topped with a huge roof that overwhelms visitors.

•05 827-898. A monk of late Silla, who spurred the development of Feng Shui principles from Tang China to Korea.
827-898. 신라 말 승려. 당나라에서 전해진 풍수지리설을 우리나라의 환경에 맞게 발전시켰다.

선암사의 연못들

선암사의 최초 창건은 통일신라 말 도선 국사[05]에 의해서라고 합니다. 그래서인지 창건과 절의 이름도 매우 풍수적입니다. 전하는 바로는 호남에 세 바위, 즉 3암이 있는데 광양 백계산 운암, 순천 조계산 선암, 영암 월출산 용암으로 도선 국사가 여기에 각각 운암사, 선암사, 용암사를 세웠다는 것입니다. 또한 선암이라는 바위는 신선이 내려준 신령한 바위로 알려져 있었는데, 그래서 선암사로 들어갈 때 건너야 하는 아름다운 홍예교의 이름은 '승선교(昇仙橋, 보물 제400호)', 즉 선계로 오르는 다리입니다. 다리를 건너면 일주문 역할을 하는 누각을 만나는데 이 누각의 이름은 '강선루(降仙樓)', 즉 신선이 내려온 누각이니, 이렇게 '승(昇)'과 '강(降)', 즉 '오름'과 '내림'을 대비시켜 그 접점이 결국 성(聖)과 속(俗)의 경계가 되게 했습니다. 강선루를 지나 일주문을 향해 걷다 보면 '삼인당(三印塘)'이라고 하는 연못을 만나게 됩니다. 이 연못은 특히 타원형의 형태를 띠고 있어 특이합니다. 한국의 전통 연못이 주로 방형(사각형)으로 된 것이 많아서 이러한 타원형의 연못은 근대기에 조성된 것 아닌가 추정되기도 했습니다. 그러나 2014년에 남원 실상사에서 이와 유사한 고려시대의 연못 시설이 발굴되면서 삼인당 역시 최소한 고려시대에 조성되었을 가능성이

높아졌습니다. '당(塘)'이라고 하는 것은 제방, 둑이라는 의미로서 삼인당이 단지 관상용에 그치는 것이 아니라 주변에서 행해졌던 경작에 물을 대는 중요한 시설이었을 가능성도 생각해볼 수 있습니다. 이곳에 머물렀던 승려들이 외부의 지원에 의존하지 않고, 사찰 주변의 경사지를 개간해 경작함으로써 자급자족하는 데 있어 이러한 제방 시설은 실용적인 역할을 겸했을 것으로 추정됩니다. 특히 삼인당 인근과 경내에도 여러 연못이 숨어 있는 점과 선암사 주변에 차밭이 경영되고 있다는 점에서 이 연못들이 단순한 감상용 그 이상의 목적을 가지고 있었음을 짐작케 합니다. 그럼에도 삼인당처럼 가운데 섬을 띄워 운치를 더했으니 참으로 세심한 손길의 결과물이라 하겠습니다. 일주문으로 올라가는 길에는 마치 원시림처럼 잘 자란 나무들이 하늘 높이 뻗어 있습니다. 때문에 일주문 안으로 들어서기 전까지는 그 너머에 있는 가람의 존재가 잘 드러나지 않습니다. 선암사의 비밀을 감추고 있는 듯한 작은 일주문은 그럼에도 커다란 지붕을 지니고 있습니다. 다른 절처럼 위압적인 금강역사상이나 사천왕은 없지만, 대신 이 커다란 지붕을 머리에 이고 있는 일주문이 방문자를 압도합니다.

Samindang, Seonam-sa Temple, Suncheon
순천 선암사 삼인당

A Private Audience with Sakyamuni Buddha

Passing *Ilju-mun* Gate and under *Beomjong-ru* Pavilion, one's path is obstructed by *Manse-ru* Pavilion, which looms large before one's eyes. On the pavilion hangs a large plaque that reads, "*Yukjogosa*(六朝古寺)," which supposedly means "Old Temple of the Sixth Patriarch," instead of the literal meaning, "Ancient Temple of the Six Dynasties."

Perhaps the sign might intend to indicate that this is a temple honoring the Sixth Patriarch Huineng. However, if this was the case, the plaque should say "*Cho*(祖)" which means "patriarch," not "*Cho*(朝)" which means "dynasty" – but it doesn't, which is curious.

Even though this question remains unsolved, if one goes around *Manse-ru* Pavilion, one will see Seonam-sa Temple's Eastern and Western Three-story Stone Pagodas(Treasure No. 395), as well as *Daeung-jeon* Hall(Treasure No. 1311), which stands between the two pagodas. While the history of Seonam-sa Temple is mainly known since the time of Master Uicheon, the Eastern and Western Three-story Stone Pagodas, which date from the Unified Silla period, tell us that its history goes further back.

The pair of stone pillars in front of *Daeung-jeon*'s stairs is for hanging Seonam-sa's "Hanging Scroll Painting of Sakyamuni Buddha"(Treasure No.1419). This scroll painting is 12.5 meters tall and was painted in 1753. The dignified figure of Sakyamuni Buddha standing in the center of the painting conveys an overwhelming presence. Yet, if one looks closely at the details, one will notice the very elaborate and fine flower pattern on Sakyamuni's *gasa*(ceremonial upper robe of a Buddhist monk). Depicted on the upper left and upper right corners of the garment are "All Buddhas of the Ten Directions" and *Dabotap* Pagoda. This scene clearly, yet simply, depicts a Dharma teaching from the *Lotus Sutra*.

The Sakyamuni Buddha enshrined in *Daeung-jeon* Hall demonstrates that, just as Master Uicheon declared in front of the pagoda enshrining the *sarira* of Great Teacher Zhiyi, this ancient temple inherited the tradition of enshrining Sakyamuni Buddha, a figure central to the *Lotus Sutra*, the core scripture of Tiantai Buddhism. The method of enshrinement is also very unique in that Sakyamuni Buddha is enshrined alone without accompanying Bodhisattvas. This is similar to the composition of the giant scroll painting mentioned earlier which depicts only Sakyamuni Buddha. Since the 1660s when Seonam-sa Temple was rebuilt, the

Daeung-jeon and Eastern and Western Three-story Stone Pagodas at Seonam-sa Temple, Suncheon
순천 선암사 대웅전과 동·서 삼층석탑

Hanging Scroll Painting of Sakyamuni Buddha, Seonam-sa, Suncheon
순천 선암사 석가모니 괘불탱

strict *Seon* tradition has been established by monks like Master Chimgoeng Hyeonbyeon[06] and his disciple, Master Hoam Yakhyu.[07] In particular, chanting was stressed, and Master Hoam recited the *Lotus Sutra* as his main form of practice. We can understand this to mean that Sakyamuni Buddha alone was considered the main Buddha. Thus, if you are in Seonam-sa's *Daeung-jeon*, you may feel as though you are in a private audience with the Buddha.

The edges of the layered brackets placed upon the pillars are ornamented with lotus flowers. There are also alternating designs of lotus flowers blooming upward from the bottom, followed by lotus buds that have not yet bloomed; above them are lotus flowers blooming downward. The bracket components on which these lotuses are carved look like the winding stems of lotus flowers. They create the illusion that all the plants are growing toward the central Buddha, as though seeking the sunlight. It is a place where, when one enters, one's mind is brought into harmony with the surroundings, and one's heart and soul are absorbed by the Buddha at the center. When looking from the front yard of *Daeung-jeon* Hall, one can see that Seonam-sa Temple has a very organized temple layout. Despite being a mountain temple, its buildings are lined up on the left and right sides of *Daeung-jeon* Hall. However, the arrangement of the grounds does not seem too rigid because, even though the overall arrangement is symmetrical, each building has a free and unrestrained appearance.

This gives the impression that as long as the buildings maintain their assigned location, they can assume any shape and form that accord with their own convenience. Therefore, Seonam-sa Temple does not feel closed off, but rather it comfortably embraces anyone who enters the space.

Sakyamuni Buddha enshrined in *Daeung-jeon*, Seonam-sa Temple
선암사 대웅전 석가모니불상

大雄殿

석가모니불과의 독대

일주문 지나 범종루 아래로 들어서면 눈앞에 길게 늘어선 만세루가 앞을 가로막습니다. 만약 "육조고사(六朝古寺)"라 적힌 큰 현판이 달려 있지 않았다면 무례하게 느껴졌을 것입니다. 육조고사. 아마도 육조 혜능 스님을 기리는 사찰이라는 뜻인 것 같은데, 그렇다면 '조(朝)'가 아닌 '조(祖)'를 썼어야 함에도 왜 저렇게 썼는지 문제를 풀어야 지나갈 수 있다는 것처럼 다가옵니다.

비록 문제는 풀지 못했어도 만세루를 돌아 들어가면 선암사 동·서 삼층석탑(보물 제395호)과 그 사이에 서 있는 대웅전(보물 제1311호)을 마주하게 됩니다. 선암사의 역사가 비록 의천 스님으로부터 본격적으로 알려지고 있지만, 통일신라시대의 동·서 삼층석탑을 통해 그 역사가 더 오래되었음을 알 수 있습니다.

대웅전 계단 앞쪽에 놓인 두 쌍의 석조지주는 선암사 석가모니불괘불탱(보물 제1419호)을 걸기 위한 것입니다. 1753년에 그려진 높이 12.5미터의 이 괘불은 중앙에서 계신 당당한 석가모니불이 압도적인 분위기로 그려졌으면서도 그 세부 묘사를 보면 가사(袈裟)의 촘촘한 꽃무늬가 정교하고 섬세하기 그지없습니다. 상단 좌우에는 오직 시방제불과 다보탑만을

묘사하여 이 장면이 『법화경』 설법 장면이라는 것을 분명하면서도 간명하게 드러낸 걸작입니다.

대웅전에 모셔진 석가모니불은 이 고찰이 의천 스님이 지의 대사 승탑 앞에서 맹세하신 바 천태종의 핵심 경전인 『법화경』의 주존 석가모니를 모신 전통을 계승하고 있음을 알려줍니다. 불상을 봉안한 방법도 특이한데 협시보살도 없이 석가모니불 한 분만 모셔져 있습니다. 선암사 괘불탱에 석가모니불만 강조하여 조성한 것과 유사합니다. 1660년대 선암사가 중건된 이후로는 침굉 현변(枕肱懸辯)[06] 스님과 그분의 제자 호암 약휴(護巖若休)[07] 스님 등에 의해 엄격한 선풍(禪風)이 확립되었습니다. 특히 염불 수행을 강조했고, 그중에서도 호암 스님은 『법화경』 염송을 수행으로 삼았다 하니 오직 석가모니불을 강조하기 위한 것으로 이해됩니다. 그래서 선암사 대웅전 안에서는 석가모니 부처님과 독대하는 기분이 듭니다.

기둥 위에 올려진 여러 단의 공포 끝은 연꽃으로 장식되었습니다. 그런데 가장 아래는 위로 핀 연꽃, 그 위는 아직 피지 않은 봉오리, 그 위는 아래로 핀 연꽃들이 번갈아 가며 나타납니다. 이

The ceiling of *Daeungbo-jeon* Hall at Seonam-sa Temple
선암사 대웅전 내부 천장

연꽃들이 새겨진 공포 부재가 마치 연꽃의
구불구불한 줄기처럼 보이면서 모든
식물이 햇빛을 찾아가듯 중앙의 부처님을
향해 자라고 있는 것처럼 보입니다. 건물
안에 들어선 사람의 마음도 이에 동화되어
마음과 정신 모두 중앙의 부처님께
흡수되는 그런 공간입니다.
이 대웅전 앞뜰에서 보면 선암사는
상당히 질서 있는 가람 배치를 보입니다.
산지 가람이라지만 대웅전을 중심으로
좌우로 늘어선 전각들이 엄격하게 도열해
있습니다. 그러나 그런 질서가 딱딱하게

느껴지지 않는 것은 비록 전체의 배치는
좌우 대칭적이지만 건물 하나하나는
자유분방한 모습을 하고 있기 때문입니다.
자리만 지킨다면 자세는 편해도 된다는
표시 같습니다. 그래서 선암사 가람은
폐쇄적이라기보다 그 공간에 들어선 사람을
자연스럽게 감싸는 느낌입니다.

- 06 1616-1684. A monk of late Joseon.
  1616-1684. 조선 후기 승려.
- 07 1664-1738. A monk of late Joseon.
  1664-1738. 조선 후기 승려.

The True Attraction of Seonam-sa Temple is Hidden Behind *Daeung-jeon* Hall

The area in front of *Daeung-jeon* Hall is indeed beautiful, but the true attraction of Seonam-sa Temple lies behind *Daeung-jeon* Hall. At a typical mountain temple, the *Daeung-jeon* Hall is located on the highest and rearmost edge of the temple grounds. In most cases, once you have seen *Daeung-jeon*, the buildings behind it have no significant meaning. But Seonam-sa Temple is different in that the hidden essence of Seonam-sa Temple begins behind *Daeung-jeon*.

In particular, the paths that guide one deeper into the back of the temple are alluring and lined by closely set buildings. Typically, high embankments and other buildings in a temple tend to block one's view, but here, you get the feeling of being drawn into another realm deeper inside the temple. In addition, the curving roof lines seem to create a rather cheerful atmosphere.

Wandering these paths behind *Daeung-jeon*, one feels as if they are freely exploring the alleyways of a country village. The annex buildings are surrounded by stone walls, and flowering trees give added harmony and a feeling of independence. That is why one feels as if they are walking through a traditional village filled with small houses. Seonam-sa Temple itself

is, after all, a small mountain village, in addition to being a small Buddha-field. Among the buildings behind *Daeung-jeon*, *Wontong-jeon* Hall clearly stands out. This building, which enshrines *Gwanseum-Bosal*(Bodhisattva Avalokitesvara of Great Compassion), is shaped like the Chinese character "丁 (*Jeong*)." Seen from the front, it looks like a crane stretching out its neck and spreading its wings wide, a splendid sight.

King Jeongjo was concerned about not having an heir, and so Great Master Nulam of Seonam-sa Temple prayed on his behalf at *Wontong-jeon* Hall; subsequently, a son was born. When the son ascended to the throne as King Sunjo,[08] he wrote and delivered a plaque with the name "*Daebokjeon*(大福田)" as an expression of gratitude. That signboard now hangs inside *Wontong-jeon* Hall. Perhaps because it was a place of prayer for the royal family, one will notice that this building is constructed in such a way that it appears to have two rooms, but is in actuality just a single room. This is also a characteristic of royal Buddhist Temple construction.

If there is a tea farm, there should also be a tea room. Though usually not open to the public, *Dharma-jeon*, which houses a water cistern, is located near the monks'

Wontong-jeon, Seonam-sa Temple
순천 선암사 원통전

Inside of *Wontong-jeon* Hall, Seonam-sa
선암사 원통전 내부

living quarters and is well-known because it has appeared in movies. Here, water flowing from the mountains is collected in four stone cisterns, and inside is equipment used to brew tea.

Last of all are the *cheukgan*, or outhouses. It is presumed they were built as early as the beginning of the 20th century, which justifies regarding them as original traditional toilets. However, contrary to the stigma surrounding traditional toilets, this facility has been visited for years by numerous monks and lay Buddhists and is surprisingly convenient and amiable, as well as eco-friendly. Before leaving the temple, one may have to discard the notion that all traditional toilets are "inconvenient."

Lastly, wherever one goes in Seonam-sa Temple they can see wonderful stone monuments, stupas, and Buddhist paintings. Moreover, as Seonam-sa Temple is now a registered UNESCO World Heritage Site, its extraordinary beauty belongs to all the people of the world and will certainly be more appreciated with the passage of time.

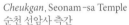

Cheukgan, Seonam-sa Temple
순천 선암사 측간

Four stone cisterns, Seonam-sa
선암사 석조

The spring scenery of Seonam-sa Temple
선암사의 봄 풍경

선암사의 진정한 매력은 대웅전 뒤편에 숨어 있다

대웅전까지의 공간도 아름답지만 선암사의
진짜 매력은 대웅전 뒤편의 사역에
있습니다. 보통 산지 가람은 대웅전이 경내
가장 위, 가장 끝자락에 자리 잡고 있습니다.
대웅전까지 보았으면 사실 그 뒤의 전각은
그리 중요한 의미를 지니지 않는 경우가
많지요. 하지만 선암사는 다릅니다.
선암사의 진정한 모습은 대웅전 뒤에서
시작됩니다.

특히 사역 뒤편으로 깊숙이 안내하는
길들은 매력적입니다. 길옆으로는 전각들이
빼곡히 늘어서 있습니다. 보통은 높은
축대나 다른 전각들로 시야가 막히기도
하지만 여기서는 저 안쪽의 또 다른 공간이
사람을 불러들이는 것 같습니다. 거기에
지붕 선이 넘실넘실 이어지는 모습은
흥겹기까지 합니다.

대웅전 뒤쪽 공간을 돌아다니다 보면 왠지
시골 마을의 골목길을 헤집고 다니는
기분이 듭니다. 부속 전각들은 별도의
돌담을 두르고 있고, 또 돌담에 어울리는
꽃나무들이 있어 더욱 독립된 공간으로
느껴집니다. 그러다 보니 아담한 집들이
모여 있는 전통 마을을 거니는 것 같습니다.
선암사는 결국 그 자체로 산속에 들어앉은
작은 마을이고, 작은 불국토(佛國土)인
셈입니다.

대웅전 뒤편 전각 중에서 단연 돋보이는
것은 원통전입니다. 관음보살을 모신 이
전각은 '정(丁)'자형 전각인데, 앞에서 보면
학 한 마리가 고개를 길게 내밀고 날개를
활짝 편 모습이어서 장관입니다.
원통전에는 정조가 아들이 없어 걱정하자
선암사의 눌암 대사가 이곳에서 기도를
올려 아들이 태어났고, 이 아들이
순조[08]로 즉위한 후 감사의 뜻으로
'대복전(大福田)'이라는 편액을 직접 써서
내려보낸 사연이 담겨 있습니다. 현재 그
현판은 건물 안에 걸려 있지요. 왕실의
기도처였던 때문인지 건물 안으로 들어서면
마치 또 하나의 방이 있는 것처럼 이중으로
구획된 것이 눈에 띕니다. 이는 왕실 원당
건축의 특징이기도 합니다.

한편 차밭이 있으니 다실도 있어야
할 것입니다. 평소 개방되지는 않지만
스님들의 요사채인 달마전의 수조 역시
영화의 배경으로 등장한 바도 있어
유명합니다. 4개의 석조 수조의 높낮이를
차례로 낮춰가며 산에서 내려오는 물을
단계적으로 받아 내리는 시설인데, 달마전
안에는 이 물로 차를 다릴 수 있는 차구가
준비되어 있습니다.

끝으로 빠뜨릴 수 없는 것이 선암사 측간,
즉 화장실입니다. 최소 1900년대 초반에는

세워졌을 것으로 보고 있으니 재래식 화장실의 원형이라 할만합니다. 하지만 재래식이라는 편견과 달리 선암사를 찾는 수많은 속인들과 스님들의 볼일을 다 받아내고 있는 이 거대한 측간은 의외로 편리하고 정감 있습니다. 더구나 친환경적이기도 하니 재래식은 무조건 불편하기만 할 것이라는 생각은 여기서 함께 버리고 가야 할 듯싶습니다.

선암사에는 이외에도 발길 닿는 곳마다 멋진 비석과 승탑, 불화 등이 가득 들어서 있습니다. 더욱이 선암사가 유네스코 세계문화유산의 하나로 등재되었으니, 그 각별한 아름다움은 이제 세계인의 것이 되어 더욱 사랑받는 사찰이 될 것임에 틀림없습니다.

●08 1790-1834. 23rd King of Joseon.
1790-1834. 조선 제23대 왕.

Daeheung-sa Temple

in Haenam County

The Layout of Daeheung-sa Temple
대흥사 가람 배치도

1	*Haetal-mun* 해탈문	8	*Gaheo-ru* 가허루	15	*Pyochungsa* 표충사
2	*Chimgye-ru* 침계루	9	*Yonghwa-dang* 용화당	16	*Josa-jeon* 조사전
3	*Myeongbu-jeon* 명부전	10	*Cheonbul-jeon* 천불전	17	*Daegwangmyeong-jeon* 대광명전
4	*Daeungbo-jeon* 대웅보전	11	Seongbo Museum 성보박물관	18	Ilji-am Hermitage 일지암
5	*Eungjin-dang · Sansin-gak* 응진당·산신각	12	*Euijung-dang* 의중당	19	Bukmireuk-am Hermitage 북미륵암
6	Three-story Stone Pagoda 삼층석탑	13	*Gangryejae* 강례제		
7	*Beomjong-gak* 범종각	14	*Boryeon-gak* 보련각		

Evolution from Foreign to Native Religion

외래종교에서 전통종교로 성장하다

Daeheung-sa Temple is also referred to as Daedun-sa Temple or "*Handeumjeol*" in native Korean. The book *Daedun saji* compiled in 1823 by the chief author, Jeong Yakyong,[01] proposes various theories in regard to the establishment of Daeheung-sa Temple.

One of the theories suggests it was established by Preceptor Ado[02] in 514, while others say it was founded by Ven. Jeonggwan from Silla in 426 and was named Manil-am Hermitage. Some say the temple was reconstructed in 508 by a monk whose dharma name is unknown; while yet another theory states that Daeheung-sa Temple was one of the temples established by Ven. Doseon after he returned from Tang China in 875 and wrote a letter of appeal to the royal court to establish 500 temples. However, those who compiled *Daedunsaji, the Record of Daedun-sa Temple*, questioned the credibility of all these theories and stated the construction of the temple took place toward the end of Unified Silla. Noting by the fact that the Three-Story Stone Pagoda(Treasure No. 320) in front of Daeheung-sa's *Eungjin-*

jeon Hall was constructed during the Unified Silla period, it then becomes clear that Daeheung-sa Temple was presumably built during late Unified Silla at the latest. Moreover, according to the *Donggukyeojiseungnam*(*Augmented Survey of the Geography of the Eastern Nation*),[03] Daeheung-sa had pagodas enshrining the *sarira* of Great Masters Sinam, Chongeun and Seongyu, believed to be from the Goryeo period. Thus, one can infer that Daeheung-sa was a regionally or perhaps even a nationally respected temple in Goryeo, but the precise period of its construction still remains uncertain. Daeheung-sa Temple rose to prominence with Great Master Seosan Cheongheo Hyujeong.[04] At the onset of the Japanese invasion of Korea, King Seonjo bestowed upon Master Hyujeong the title *Paldo-do-chongseop*.[05] This prompted Master Hyujeong and his disciples Ven. Yujeong, Ven. Cheoyeong, and Ven. Yeonggyu to organize a militia of monk warriors, ultimately culminating in a turning point in the war against the Japanese invasion.

대흥사는 대둔사, 또는 순우리말로
'한듬절'이라고도 불렸습니다.
정약용•⁰¹을 필두로 1823년 편찬된
『대둔사지(大芚寺誌)』에는 대흥사 창건에
관한 다양한 설들이 정리되어 있습니다.
514년 아도 화상•⁰²의 창건설, 426년 신라
정관 스님이 창건하여 만일암이라 했다는
기록, 508년에 법명을 알 수 없는 한 스님이
중건하였다는 설, 그리고 875년에 도선
스님이 당나라에서 귀국하여 500개의
사찰을 세울 것을 상소한 가운데 대흥사도
포함되어 있었다는 설 등이 전해집니다.
그러나 『대둔사지』의 편찬자들은
이러한 설들의 신빙성이 낮다고 보고
통일신라시대 말엽에 창건된 것으로
추정했습니다. 경내 응진전 앞에 있는
통일신라시대의 대흥사 삼층석탑(보물
제320호)을 보면 대흥사는 최소한 통일신라
후기에는 이미 창건되었을 것입니다.
또한 『동국여지승람』•⁰³에는 대흥사에
고려시대 승려로 추정되는 신암, 총은,
성유 등 세 스님의 부도가 있었다고
전하고 있어 고려시대에도 이 지역에서
혹은 국가적으로 비중 있는 사찰이었음을

짐작할 수 있지만 정확한 창건 시점을
알기는 어려운 상황입니다.
그러던 대흥사가 주요한 무대로 등장한
것은 서산대사 청허 휴정 스님•⁰⁴
때부터입니다. 임진왜란이 발발하자
선조는 휴정 스님에게 팔도도총섭•⁰⁵이라는
중책을 맡겼고, 이에 스님은 제자 유정,
처영, 영규와 함께 승군을 일으켜
임진왜란에 큰 전기를 마련했습니다.

•01   1762-1836. Confucian scholar of the late Joseon
      period.
      1762-1836. 조선 후기 유학자.

•02   A Goguryeo Buddhist Master who propagated
      Buddhism in the Silla period.
      신라에 불교를 전파한 고구려 승려.

•03   Documents the geography and customs of each
      province in Joseon during King Seongjong's reign.
      조선 성종 때 각 도의 지리, 풍속 등을 기록한
      우리나라 지리서.

•04   1520-1604. A renowned Buddhist Master of the
      Joseon period.
      1520-1604. 조선 시대 고승.

•05   Do-chongseop refers to the highest position given to
      members of the Sangha during the Joseon Dynasty.
      도총섭이란 조선시대에 나라에서 내렸던 승려에 대한
      직책 중 최고 승직을 말한다.

Master Hyujeong spent most of his life on Mt. Myohyang-san, but he is thought to have practiced at Daeheung-sa during his early years as a monk. During the Japanese invasion, he utilized Daeheung-sa Temple as the headquarters and led his monk militia from this temple. He must have immediately realized the geographic importance of Daeheung-sa Temple during this process. Prior to his Parinirvana on Mt. Myohyang-san, he implored that his robe and alms bowl be bequeathed to Daeheung-sa Temple and made a formal entreaty for an annual memorial ritual. His gift of robe and alms bowl signified Daeheung-sa Temple as the new center of Buddhism in Joseon.

What value did Great Master Hyujeong see in Daeheung-sa Temple? It is hard to know exactly why he deemed Daeheung-sa Temple so important, but one can certainly see the impact of his foresight. First and foremost, up until the Japanese invasion, terraced farmland was considered advantageous as a means of conserving water. As irrigation technology developed, however, the vast plains of the Honam region emerged as a key economic resource for the production of food. Thus, it appears that Master Hyujeong possessed a keen economic insight.

Secondly, Haenam County was known as a place of exile for Joseon intellectuals. Historical figures like Wongyo Lee Gwangsa,[06] Dasan Jeong Yakyong, and Chusa Kim Jeonghui[07] spent years in exile in the Honam region. Master Hyujeong encouraged interaction between the monastics and advanced scholars, and these interpersonal relations played a crucial role in helping Buddhism outgrow its reputation as a foreign religion and establish itself as a native Korean religion. Undoubtedly, his political insight made this transformation possible.

Buddhism became widely respected in Korea thanks to Master Hyujeong's foresight and consequently, Daeheung-sa Temple also began assuming a greater role. Daeheung-sa produced thirteen Great Patriarchs as well as thirteen great master instructors who spearheaded the growth of Buddhism in Joseon. This accomplishment might have been somewhat overshadowed by the fact that sixteen National Preceptors were produced in Songgwang-sa Temple during the Goryeo Dynasty, but Daeheung-sa Temple can still be regarded as Joseon's treasured Buddhist temple representing the Jewel of Sangha that is at the epitome of the history of Buddhism in the Joseon period.

清虛堂休淨大師

Daeheung-sa
해남 대흥사

Stupa of Great Master Seosan at Daeheung -sa Temple, Haenam (Treasure No.1347)
해남 대흥사 서산대사탑(보물 제1347호)

휴정 스님은 묘향산에서 대부분의 일생을 보냈지만 출가 초창기에 대흥사에서 수행을 했다고 합니다. 특히 임진왜란 중에는 대흥사를 승군(僧軍)의 본영으로 삼아 진두지휘하였습니다. 이 과정에서 대흥사의 지리적 중요성을 단번에 알아챈 것으로 보입니다. 스님은 묘향산에서 입적하시기 전에 자신의 발우와 가사를 대흥사에 전할 것이며, 그곳에서 1년에 한 번씩 제사를 지낼 것까지 꼼꼼하게 당부했다고 합니다. 의발(衣鉢)을 전한다는 것은 그곳이 조선불교의 새로운 중심이 된다는 의미입니다.

휴정 스님은 왜 이토록 대흥사를 중요시했을까요? 그 의중을 정확히 읽어낼 수는 없지만 결과적으로 어떤 일이 일어났는지는 확인해 볼 수 있습니다. 우선 임진왜란 이전까지만 해도 계단식 경작지가 물을 관리하기 유리했습니다. 그러나 점차 물 대는 기술이 발전하면서 호남 지역의 평야가 대규모 경작지로서 새로운 경제력으로 부각되기 시작했습니다.

스님의 높은 경제적 안목이 짐작됩니다. 두 번째로는 이후 이곳 해남 지역은 많은 조선 지식인들의 유배지로 유명했습니다. 원교 이광사[06], 다산 정약용, 추사 김정희[07] 같은 분들이 이곳에서 유배 생활을 했습니다. 스님은 제자들이 진정한 지식인과 교류하길 바라셨고, 실제로 이러한 교류는 점차 불교가 조선에서 외래종교의 이미지를 벗고 전통종교로 받아들여지는 데 결정적인 역할을 했습니다. 스님의 높은 정치적 안목이 엿보이는 대목입니다.

그러한 미래 설계 덕분인지 조선불교의 위상은 크게 달라졌고 그만큼 대흥사의 역할도 커졌습니다. 대흥사에서는 조선불교를 이끌어 간 걸출한 13인의 대종사와 13인의 대강사를 배출했습니다. 송광사가 고려시대 16인의 국사를 배출한 것에 다소 가려졌지만, 대흥사는 그야말로 조선의 승보사찰이라 하겠으며 그 자체로서 조선불교의 역사가 된 것입니다.

• 06 1705-1777. Literary figure of Late Joseon.
      1705-1777. 조선 후기의 문인.

• 07 1786-1856. A theoretician, calligrapher, and painter
      of Late Joseon.
      1786-1856. 조선 말기의 문신.

Three Compounds of Daeheung-sa Temple

Like Tongdo-sa and Magok-sa Temples, Daeheung-sa Temple is composed of three distinct areas. However, their arrangement is somewhat different. At Tongdo-sa Temple, the temple buildings are grouped closely together yet arranged in an orderly manner. At Magok-sa Temple, the temple areas are arranged in a free and unrestrained manner, yet they organically harmonize as one cohesive unit. Daeheung-sa Temple, on the other hand, consists of independent temple compounds, separated from each other and arranged as if they were separate temples.

The temple areas are divided into the northern compound, southern compound, and annex compound. Each compound is centered on *Daeungbo-jeon* Hall, *Cheonbul-jeon* Hall, and *Pyochungsa*,[08] respectively. The northern *Daeungbo-jeon* Hall area is the center, and the two other compounds are located below it to the south. However, from a spatial

대흥사의 삼원

perspective, the *Cheonbul-jeon* area can also be viewed as the center, with the *Daeungbo-jeon* Hall and *Pyochungsa* areas located left and right facing the center. Although the three compounds have been freely arranged, each area of the temple can appear as the center depending on what perspective one views the temple from. Such a free spatial arrangement can be said to be a means of maintaining an organic personality between the areas while also maximizing each area's independence.

통도사와 마곡사와 마찬가지로 대흥사 역시 세 개의 원으로 구성되어 있지만 결합 방식은 다릅니다. 통도사는 가까이 있으되 질서정연하게 나란히 배치되었고, 마곡사는 다소 자유분방하게 자리 잡고 있지만 서로 유기적으로 호응하며 하나를 이루고 있습니다. 이와는 달리 대흥사는 각각 독립적인 원으로 구성하여 서로 일정한 거리를 두고 떨어져서 서로 별개의 절인 것처럼 배치되었습니다.

세 원은 북원, 남원, 별원으로 나뉘는데, 각각 대웅보전, 천불전, 표충사*[08]를 중심 전각으로 합니다. 북쪽 대웅보전 영역이 중심이 되어 그 아래 남쪽으로 두 원이 배치되었다고 볼 수 있습니다. 하지만 공간적 측면에서 보자면 천불전 영역을 중심으로 대웅보전 영역과 표충사 영역이 중심을 향해 좌우에 배치된 모습으로 볼 수도 있습니다. 이렇듯 세 원이 자유롭게 배치되었으나 어떤 입장에서 보느냐에 따라 각각 가장 중요한 위치가 되니, 이 배치의 자유로움은 서로의 유기적 성격을 유지하면서도 독립성을 최대한 이끌어내기 위한 방편이라 하겠습니다.

◁ Daeheung-sa Temple, Haenam
해남 대흥사

• 08 *Pyochungsa* is a shrine dedicated mainly to Great *Seon* Master Hyujeong, along with Ven. Yujeong and Ven. Cheoyeong.
표충사는 휴정 선사와 유정·처영 스님을 모신 사당이다.

Chimgye-ru Pavilion and *Shimjin-Gyo* Bridge, Daeheung-sa
대흥사 침계루와 심진교

The Northern Compound

Among the buildings of Daeheung-sa Temple, which are arranged north to south, the northern compound is thought to have been built first. If the terrain had been higher in the north, the northern compound would have been the highest, most central area and therefore, the center of Daeheung-sa Temple. However, that is not the case. Visitors enter the temple from west to east, and the terrain is lower in the north. Hence, the northern compound does not appear to be the center of the temple.

The sublime northern compound sits behind Geumdang Stream. After crossing *Shimjin-gyo* Bridge, meaning "searching for the truth," one finds the magnificent *Chimgye-ru* Pavilion. The signboard for this pavilion was written by Lee Gwangsa. Lee Gwangsa's father was exiled after criticizing the political faction known as *Noron*,[09] impeding his political career. To make matters worse, Lee Gwangsa was later involved in the Eulhae Purge[10] and exiled for life. In exile, he soothed his grudge through study and calligraphy. His calligraphy style was based on the Wang Xizhi style of Kim Saeng, a famous calligrapher of Silla period. But, at the same time, he created his own unique calligraphy style that incorporated intense curves to express his passion. It is said that,

after he was banished to Sinji-do Island in Haenam, nearby temples endeavored to receive handwritten signboards from him. Not only was his calligraphy style unique and beautiful, but the curvature of the Chinese characters resembled waves, and therefore were popular as it was believed they could protect temples from fires.

The main hall in the northern compound is *Daeungbo-jeon* Hall, which has a grand appearance featuring five *kan*s on its front side and a hip-and-gable roof. The hall enshrines the Seated Sakyamuni Buddha Triad(Treasure No. 1863), with Sakyamuni Buddha sitting between Amitabha Buddha and Bhaisajyaguru Buddha. The statues of the Buddhas on the left and right sides were created by Master Taejeon in 1612, and Sakyamuni Buddha in the center was enshrined later; it is larger in size and slightly different in style.

Daeungbo-jeon is said to have been rebuilt in 1667 by Master Simsu over a span of three years. The interior of the hall is magnificent with a variety of decor. The columns look like trees taken directly from the forest, adding a natural beauty to the hall.

북원

남-북 가람 배치에서 북쪽에 위치한 북원은 아마도 대흥사에서 제일 먼저 터를 잡은 사역으로 생각됩니다. 그러나 만약 지형이 북쪽으로 갈수록 높아지는 형상이라면 북원이 가장 안쪽 높은 곳이 되어 대흥사의 중심 영역이 되겠지만 실제 지형은 그렇지 않습니다. 진입로는 서에서 동으로 놓여 있고, 지대도 북쪽이 낮기 때문에 북원이 중심인 것처럼 보이지는 않습니다.

금당천 너머 북원은 장중합니다. '진리를 찾는다'는 의미의 심진교(尋眞橋)를 건너면 웅장한 침계루가 버티고 서 있습니다. 침계루 편액은 이광사의 글씨입니다. 이광사의 부친은 노론[09]을 탄핵하다 유배되어 아들인 이광사의 벼슬길도 막혔고, 설상가상 나주벽서사건[10]에 연루되어 본인도 죽을 때까지 풀리지 못한 유배를 떠나게 되었습니다. 대신 그는 울분을 학문과 서예로 달랬지요. 특히 그의 서체는 신라시대 명필 김생의 왕희지체를 바탕으로 하고 있습니다. 그러면서도 자신의 격정을 더욱 격렬하게 구불구불 담아낸 그만의 서체를 탄생시켰습니다. 마침 그가 해남 신지도에 유배되는 바람에 근처의 사찰들은 명필 이광사의 편액을 받으려 부단히 노력했다고 합니다. 서체도 독특하고 아름다우려니와 구불구불한 형상이 마치 물결과 같아

절의 화재를 막아준다고도 해서 인기가 높았습니다.

북원의 중심 전각은 팔작지붕을 얹은 정면 5칸의 웅장한 자태를 지닌 대웅보전입니다. 대웅보전에 모셔진 불상은 석가모니불을 중심으로 좌우에 아미타불과 약사불을 모신 삼세불상(보물 제1863호)입니다. 좌우 부처님은 1612년에 태전 스님이 조성한 것입니다. 중앙의 석가모니 부처님은 그 후에 재차 봉안한 불상인데 크기도 더 크고 양식도 조금 다릅니다. 대웅보전은 1667년에 심수 스님이 3년에 걸쳐 중건한 것이라 합니다. 법당 내부는 질서정연하고 다양한 장엄으로 화려한데 기둥들은 숲에서 자라던 나무를 그대로 옮겨온 듯 휘어져 있어 자연스러움을 살렸습니다.

[09] A political faction in late Joseon.
조선 후기의 정파.

[10] A conspiracy that occurred in 1755 in late Joseon. It was related to an incident where a civil official named Yoon Ji posted a piece of writing on the wall of Naju Inn. Referred to as Naju mural case or Writing on the Wall Case (Naju Gwaeseo Sageon).
1755년 조선 후기 문신인 윤지가 나주 객사에 붙인 벽서와 관련해 일어난 역모 사건.

Three Buddha Statues
of Sakyamuni in
Daeungbo-jeon,
Daeheung-sa Temple
해남 대흥사 대웅보전
석가여래삼불좌상

Daeungbo-jeon at Daeheung-sa Temple
해남 대흥사 대웅보전

A Tale of Two Writers on the Signboard
of *Daeungbo-jeon* Hall at Daeheung-sa Temple

대흥사 대웅보전 현판에 얽힌 두 문인 이야기

The signboard for *Daeungbo-jeon* Hall was written by Lee Gwangsa, and here is the story behind it. When Chusa Kim Jeonghui stopped by Daeheung-sa Temple on his way to exile in 1840, he criticized the calligraphy on the sign as "too weak and secular." He offered to write a new one on condition that the old one be removed, after which he gave the temple the "*Muryangsu-gak*(無量壽閣)" signboard. Kim Jeonghui had always criticized Lee Gwangsa's calligraphy style, saying, "His understanding of the calligraphy styles of Yan Zehnqing and Ouyang Xun is superficial." Although he claimed to have seen the copybook of Wang Xizhi's style, he took it for granted without critically reviewing mistakes." He even ridiculed Lee Gwangsa by saying, "He does not even know how to hold a writing brush." It is likely that Kim Jeonghui criticized Lee Gwangsa so harshly because his calligraphy style is eruptive and intemperately conveys his emotions into the characters. However, Chusa Kim Jeonghui, who spent most of his life in exile before returning to Hanyang(Seoul's former name), visited Daeheung-sa Temple on his way home to look again at Lee Gwangsa's signboard. He then admitted that his previous criticisms had been a mistake. He likely made this confession because he had come to understand the source of Lee Gwangsa's anger and resentment.

대흥사 대웅보전 현판도 역시 이광사의 글씨입니다. 이 현판에 얽힌 이야기가 있습니다. 추사 김정희가 1840년 유배길에 대흥사를 들렀을 때 이 현판을 보고 '힘이 없고 속기가 흐른다'며 현판을 내릴 것을 당부하고 대신 자신이 글을 써 주겠다며 '무량수각' 현판을 남겼다고 합니다.
김정희는 평소 이광사의 글씨에 대해 '안진경체와 구양순체는 겉만 알고 있으며 왕희지 법첩을 보았다지만 그 오류 검증도 안 하고 받아들인' 데다가 심지어 '붓 잡는 법도 모른다'고 비판했습니다. 이렇게까지 비판했던 이유는 아마 이광사의 글씨가 자신의 감정을 있는 그대로 폭발시키듯 드러낸 외향적인 글씨였기 때문이 아닌가 싶습니다. 그러나 거의 평생을 유배지에서 보내다 해배되어 한양으로 올라가던 추사는 다시 대흥사에 들러 이광사의 현판을 찾았다고 합니다. 그리고 한때 자신의 비판이 잘못된 것이었음을 시인했다고 하니, 아마 이광사의 그 분노와 울분이 어디서 비롯되었는지 그도 비로소 체감했기 때문일 것입니다.

The Southern Compound

In the southern compound, *Bonghyang-gak* and *Yonghwa-dang* are located on the left and right sides of *Cheonbul-jeon* Hall(Treasure No. 1807), and *Gaheo-ru* Pavilion stands at the front. This compound is Daeheung-sa's monastic college for Buddhist tenets, and perhaps is where the temple's thirteen master instructors were produced through comprehensive training and cultivation. It is interesting how *Gaheo-ru*, the entrance to the southern compound, has "*ru*" in its name although it is not a pavilion. *Gaheo* means "riding the empty space," which allow visitors to regard "empty space"(*heo*) as the invisible first floor. Indeed, this double entendre conveys a *hwadu*, or *koan*, that the *Gaheo-ru* entrance is actually "floating on air." The One Thousand Buddhas enshrined in *Cheonbul-jeon* Hall have a special history. *Cheonbul-jeon* Hall was rebuilt in 1813 under the leadership of Master Punggye. He wanted to enshrine Buddhas made of zeolite from Gyeongju, but carving them took six years. The Thousand Buddhas were then loaded onto two ships sailing to Haenam via Busan. However, one ship was blown off course in a storm and landed in Nagasaki, Japan, finally returning safely in August 1818. Upon hearing this story, Dasan Jeong Yakyong suggested writing "日"(*Il*) on each statue to commemorate this special event. In fact, many of the One Thousand Buddha statues at Daeheung-sa Temple have "*Il*" for "*Ilbon*(designating or signifying Japan)", written in red. The story is told in the book *Record of Drifting to Japan*(*Ilbon Pyohaerok*) by Master Punggye. It is fascinating as it offers insight into the zeolite Buddha statues enshrined in the temple and marine transportation between Joseon and Japan at the time.

One Thousand Buddha statues in
Cheonbul-jeon at Daeheung-sa Temple
해남 대흥사 천불전 천불상

남원

남원은 천불전(보물 제1807호)을 중심으로 봉향각과 용화당이 좌우에 늘어서고, 앞에는 가허루가 놓여 있습니다. 이 공간은 대흥사의 강원에 해당합니다. 아마도 13대 강사는 이곳에서의 철저한 훈련과 수행의 결과로 만들어졌을 것입니다.

남원으로 들어가는 입구인 가허루(駕虛樓)는 사실 누각 형식이 아님에도 '누'인 것이 재미있습니다. '가허(駕虛)'는 '허공에 올라탔다'는 뜻이니 여기에서는 보이지 않는 1층을 '허(虛)'로 만들어 "사실은 지금 떠 있음"이라고 화두를 던지는 듯합니다.

천불전에 모셔진 천불에는 특별한 사연이 있습니다. 천불전은 1813년에 중건 되었는데 이를 이끈 풍계 스님이 천불을 경주 불석으로 모시고 싶어 6년 동안의 불사 끝에 모두 조성하였습니다.

일을 마치자 두 척의 배에 천불을 나누어 싣고 부산을 거쳐 해남으로 향했는데, 중간에 풍랑을 만나 그만 배 한 척이 일본 나가사키까지 표류했다가 1818년 8월 겨우 무사히 돌아오게 되었습니다. 정약용은 이 이야기를 듣고 "천불 중에서 이렇게 일본에 다녀오신 부처님께는 '일(日)' 자를 새겨 이 특별한 사건을 기록에 남기라"고 충고했는데, 실제 천불 중에는 붉은색으로 '일' 혹은 '일본'이라 쓰여진 불상이 다수 전합니다. 이 이야기의 전말은 풍계 스님이 지은 『일본표해록』에 전하는데, 당시 불석으로 모신 불상에 대한 인식, 일본과의 해상교통 등을 엿볼 수 있어 매우 흥미로운 자료입니다.

Cheonbul-jeon Hall, Daeheung-sa Temple
해남 대흥사 천불전

Annex Compound

The annex compound is a place honoring Master Seosan Hyujeong, Samyeong Yujeong, and Noimuk Cheoyeong who saved Joseon by leading a monk militia when Japan invaded Korea in 1592. *Pyochungsa*, the compound's central shrine, was built in 1788 during the 12th year of King Jeongjo's reign. Hence, it was the last area to be built at Daeheung-sa Temple.

There is also a Sanctuary and a temple named Pyochung-sa located in Miryang. They are dedicated to Seosan Hyujeong, Samyeong Yujeong, and Giheo Yeonggyu, and like Daeheung-sa Temple, it too is composed of a Buddhist area and *Pyochungsa*, a Confucian area. The coexistence of a Buddhist temple(*sawon*) and Confucian shrine(*sadang*), such as at Daeheung-sa Temple and Pyochung-sa Temple in Miryang, means that Buddhism and Confucianism recognized and accepted each other. In particular, the establishment of a ritual space, *sa*(祠), inside the temple by royal authority means that Joseon had changed its perception of Buddhism. This achievement, of course, is the result of strenuous devotion to the country displayed by Buddhist monks who risked their lives in the face of national crises, such as the Japanese invasion of Korea. This was only possible after many years and the sacrifice of many lives. *Pyochungsa* stands as a testament to the fact that that the current traditional status of Buddhism in Korea did not come without sacrifices.

One can enter the *Pyochungsa* area through the three-gated(*soseulsammun*) *Hoguk-mun* Gate, which features a middle gate that is higher than the other two. Inside the area stands a five *kan* building called *Uijung-dang*, with *Gangryejae* and *Boryeon-gak* on the left and right sides facing each other. The *Uijung-dang* area is for ritual preparation. One can enter the shrine area after passing through a second gate called *Yeje-mun* Gate, also consisting of three gates(*soseulsammun*). *Pyochungsa*, which is the main building in the annex area, is small in size and may be considered a supplementary space. However, during Joseon, when ancestral rites were considered extremely important, the standard for a shrine was three *kan*s. Instead, the prestige of this shrine is revealed through the "*Pyochungsa*(表忠祠)" signboard, written and presented by King Jeongjo. The big lavish calligraphy that fills the sign, in comparison to the size of the building, reflects the character of King Jeongjo. Located deep in the annex compound is *Daegwangmyeong-jeon* Hall, which was built by Chusa Kim Jeonghui's friend

Seon Master Choui,[*11] Kim Jeonghui's disciple Shin Kwanho and Heo Ryeon. It was constructed as an offering for Master Chusa's release from exile. It is believed that Seon Master Choui painted the Eleven-Faced Bodhisattva Avalokitesvara and Bodhisattva Cundi Avalokitesvara, which are both now displayed in the Seongbo Museum. Considering that these were paintings also drawn for Chusa Kim Jeonghui, Daeheung-sa Temple is imbued with friendship transcending animosity between Confucianism and Buddhism during the Joseon period.

Pyochungsa, Daeheung-sa Temple, Haenam
해남 대흥사 표충사

별원

별원은 임진왜란 당시 승병을 일으켜 조선을 구한 서산 휴정과 사명 유정, 그리고 뇌묵 처영 스님을 기리는 공간입니다. 중심 전각인 표충사는 정조 12년인 1788년에 세워졌기 때문에 대흥사의 삼원 중에서 가장 나중에 만들어진 공간입니다. 표충사란 이름의 사당과 절은 밀양에도 있는데 그곳은 서산 휴정과 사명 유정, 그리고 기허 영규를 기리는 곳으로 대흥사와 마찬가지로 불교적 공간과 함께 표충사(表忠祠)라는 유교적 공간으로 구성되어 있습니다. 이처럼 대흥사와 밀양의 표충사처럼 불교적 공간인 사원(寺院)과 유교적 공간인 사당(祠堂)이 함께 자리한다는 것은 불교와 유교가 서로를 인정하고 받아들였음을 의미한다고 볼 수 있습니다. 특히 사찰 안에 사(祠)라는 제사 공간이 국가 차원에서 설치된 것은 조선이 불교를 인식하는 방식이 획기적으로 변화했음을 의미합니다. 이러한 성과는 물론 임진왜란과 같은 국가적 위기 상황에서 불교가 분연히 일어나 목숨을 걸고 나라를 위해 헌신한 결과입니다.

Inside of *Pyochungsa*, Daeheung-sa Temple
대흥사 표충사 내부

이렇게 되기까지 오랜 시간이 걸렸고, 많은 피를 흘린 다음에야 가능했습니다. 표충사는 불교가 지금처럼 전통으로 자리잡게 된 것이 결코 거저 이루어진 것이 아님을 웅변하고 있는 장소입니다. 표충사 영역은 솟을삼문 형식으로 된 호국문을 통해 들어섭니다. 그 안에는 축선을 들어서 의중당이라는 5칸짜리 건물이 펼쳐지고, 그 좌우로는 강례재와 보련각이 마주보고 있습니다. 이 공간이 일종의 제사 준비 공간이라면, 여기에서 다시 예제문이라는 두 번째 솟을삼문을 지나 사당 영역에 들어서게 됩니다. 남원과 북원의 중심 전각이 거대한 불전이었던 것에 비해 별원의 핵심인 표충사는 규모가 작아 부수적 공간으로 생각할 수도 있지만, 제사를 그토록 중요하게 생각했던 조선에서도 사당의 표준은 3칸이었습니다. 대신 이 건물의 위용은 정조가 직접 써서 내린 '표충사' 편액을 통해서 드러납니다. 건물의 규모에 비해 커다란 현판 가득히 채워진 호방한 글씨가 정조의 성격을 잘 반영하는 듯합니다.

별원의 옆으로 더 깊이 들어간 곳에 자리한 대광명전은 추사 김정희의 친구인 초의 선사[11]와 제자인 신관호, 허련이 추사가 유배에서 풀려나기를 기원하면서 지은 것이었습니다. 초의 선사는 지금은 성보박물관에 걸려 있는 십일면관음보살도와 준제관음보살도를 그린 것으로도 추정되는데, 이 역시 추사를 위해 그린 것이라 하니 곳곳에 유불(儒佛)을 초월한 우정이 배어 있습니다.

• 11 1786-1866. The 13th Patriarch of Daeheung-sa Temple who established the Korean tea ceremony (茶道).
1786-1866. 대흥사 제13대 종사로 다도(茶道)의 정립자이다.

Statue of Master Choui
초의 동상

The Tea-scented Hermitage, Ilji-am

Seon Master Choui is the one who elevated the reputation of Joseon tea over that of Chinese tea, which most intellectuals preferred. Yet, it was not merely his skilled roasting and preparation of the tea that enabled his social interactions with the greatest intellectuals of the time. Rather, what should be credited is his wealth of erudition and profound understanding of Buddhism, which even convinced intellectuals and Confucian scholars(*Yu-ja*). On one occasion, Master Choui debated *Seon* with Master Baekpa Geungseon,[12] a debate now regarded as one of the most important in the history of Joseon Buddhism.

Ilji-am Hermitage is where the influence of *Seon* Master Choui has been studied in depth and is treasured. Master Choui rebuilt Iljiam Hermitage in 1842 and stayed there until he entered Parinirvana in 1866. It is about a 10-minute walk from Daeheung-sa Temple. Here, he wrote two books on the style of tea in Joseon period:

Ilji-am Hermitage, Daeheung-sa Temple, Haenam
해남 대흥사 일지암

Dongdasong and *Dasinjeon*. Although the temple is small in size, it reminds one of Monet's famous impressionist painting "The Artist's Garden at Giverny." First, there is a small thatched-roof cottage, and above a pond in front of it is a loft supported by layered stone pillars. This is where Master Choui coined the phrase *Daseonilmi*, which refers to the single exquisite flavor of tea and meditative stabilization(*Samadhi*) or *Seon*. This inspired the calligraphic masterpiece *Myeongseon* by Chusa Kim Jeonghui. Chusa wrote this while exiled on Jeju Island in return for tea sent by Master Choui; *Myeongseon* was another pseudonym of Master Choui. Although Chusa Kim Junghui's masterpiece is no longer at Daeheung-sa Temple, his memorial tablet '*Illohyangsil*(一爐香室)' remains. His masterpiece evokes a scene of tea boiling on a brazier and its fragrance permeating the air.

An hour-long walk from Ilji-am takes one to Bukmireuk-am, where one can see the Rock-Carved Seated Buddha(National Treasure No. 308), a masterpiece dating from the Unified Silla period. Its distinctiveness

The signboard, *Illohyangsil*(一爐香室)
일로향실 편액

lies in the fact that despite being carved rather shallowly, it appears to be carved in high relief. Its solemn body gives it overwhelming dignity.

Heavenly beings offering lotus and incense to Buddha are elegantly seated on his knee. Moreover, the heavenly beings look alive, soaring into the air and seeming to urge us to join in this offering to Buddha. Thus, the dynamic illustrations on the surface are so vivid that they seem to exist right in front your eyes. The perseverance of whoever constructed these is more than remarkable because he climbed deep into the mountains, sculpted this enormous Buddha, and built two stone pagodas beside it.

Only religious aspiration could motivate one to undertake such an extraordinary project. Buddhism, which originated in India, had to overcome many obstacles for a long time before it would be accepted in Korea. However, Buddhism eventually became accepted as a native Korean religion, standing firmly and proudly representing Korean religious tradition in mountains just like this pagoda.

Rock-carved Seated Buddha at Bukmireuk-am Hermitage of Daeheung-sa Temple, Haenam
해남 대흥사 북미륵암 마애여래좌상

차향이 배인 암자, 일지암

초의 선사는 당시 대부분의 지식인들이
중국 차를 선호할 때 조선 차의 경지를 그
이상으로 끌어올린 분입니다. 그러나 초의
선사가 단지 차를 잘 덖고 잘 만들었다는
이유만으로 당대 최고의 지식인들과 교류한
것은 아니었습니다. 그것은 그의 풍부한
학식과 유자(儒者)들도 설득시켰던 그의
불교에 대한 깊은 이해 덕분입니다. 일찍이
백파 긍선 스님[12]과 선(禪)에 관한 논쟁을
벌인 바 있는데 이것은 조선 후기 불교사에
있어 매우 중요한 논쟁으로 손꼽힙니다.
그런 초의 선사의 흔적을 가장 깊게 우려내
간직하고 있는 곳이 일지암입니다. 초의
선사는 대흥사에서 걸어서 10여 분 정도면
도달하는 일지암을 1842년에 중건하여
1866년 입적할 때까지 머물렀습니다.
그리고 이곳에서 『동다송(東茶頌)』,
『다신전(茶神傳)』과 같은 조선 차에 대한
책을 저술했습니다. 규모는 단출하지만
아담한 초당 한 채와 그 앞의 연못 위에
돌을 켜켜이 쌓아 기둥을 만들어 자그마한
누를 올린 자우홍련사는 마치 인상파
화가인 모네의 유명한 지베르니의 정원을
보는 듯합니다. 여기서 초의 선사가
강조한 다선일미(茶禪一味), 즉 차와 선이
서로 통한다는 말은 추사 김정희의 걸작
'명선(茗禪)'을 탄생시켰습니다. 추사는

제주도 유배 기간 중 초의 선사가 보내준
차에 대한 보답으로 이 글씨를 썼습니다.
"명선"은 초의 선사의 또 다른 호이기도
합니다.
추사의 '명선'은 지금은 대흥사를 떠났지만,
김정희의 편액인 "일로향실(一爐香室)"이
대흥사에 남아 있습니다. 방 안에 둔
향로에서 끓인 차의 향이 그윽하게
퍼져 가득한 모습이 그의 글씨를 통해
시각화되었습니다.

일지암에서 다시 1시간여를 걸어 올라가면 북미륵암에 다다릅니다. 여기에서는 통일신라시대의 걸작 마애여래좌상(국보 제308호)을 만날 수 있습니다. 얕게 파냈으면서도 마치 깊게 양각된 것처럼 보이며, 매우 장중한 신체가 그대로 압도적인 위엄으로 다가오는 것이 특징입니다.

Heavenly beings of Rock-carved Seated Buddha at Bukmireuk-am Hermitage
북미륵암 마애여래좌상의 천인들

부처님 주변에서 한쪽 무릎을 꿇고 앉아 열렬한 마음으로 연꽃과 향을 공양 올리는 천인들의 모습은 유려하기 그지없습니다. 더욱이 공중에 솟아올라 마치 우리를 바라보며 이 공양에 동참할 것을 호소하는 듯한 비천은 모두 살아 있는 존재처럼 느껴집니다. 이렇게 전면에 걸쳐 역동적으로 표현된 상(象)들은 지금 내 앞에 실제로 나타난 존재인 듯 생생합니다. 이 땅끝 깊은 산중에 올라 이토록 거대한 마애불을 새기고 그 주변에는 석탑도 2기나 세웠으니 이를 조성한 이의 집념이 놀랍기만 합니다.

종교적 열망이 아니라면 누구도 이런 무모한 일은 하지 않았을 것입니다. 저 멀리 인도에서 출발한 불교가 해동 조선에서 전통으로 인정받은 과정은 그보다 몇 배나 더 길고 어려웠지만 결국에는 이 탑처럼 우리 산속에 전통의 이름으로 우뚝 서게 되었습니다.

•12 1767-1852.

261

Time Line

연보

This time line includes facts regarding the seven mountain temples introduced in this book, as well as other UNESCO World Heritage Sites in Korea, such as Haein-sa Temple's *Janggyeong Pan-jeon* Repositories for the Tripitaka Koreana Woodblocks, Seokgur-am Hermitage and Bulguk-sa Temple.

이 연보에는 이 책에 소개된 산사 일곱 곳과 더불어 한국의 또다른 유네스코 세계유산인 해인사(장경판전, 팔만대장경), 석굴암·불국사에 관련된 내용도 포함되어 있습니다.

529	Establishment of Seonam-sa Temple, formerly known Haecheon-sa Temple, by Great Master Ado of Goguryeo (speculation) 고구려 아도 화상 해천사(선암사의 전신) 창건설		의상 대사, 당나라 침공 첩보를 가지고 신라로 귀국 의상 대사, 양양에서 관음보살 친견하고 낙산사 창건
553	Establishment of Beopju-sa Temple by Spiritual Patriarch Uisin of Silla (speculation) 신라 의신 조사에 의한 법주사 창건설	672	Establishment of Bongjeong-sa Temple by Master Uisang and his disciple Neungin 의상 대사, 제자 능인과 봉정사 창건
640	Establishment of Magok-sa Temple by Great Master Jajang (speculation) 자장 율사 마곡사 창건설	676	Establishment of Buseok-sa Temple by Master Uisang 의상 대사, 부석사 창건
643	Great Master Jajang of Silla returns from his studies in Tang China 신라 자장 율사, 당나라 유학 마치고 귀국	740(or 762)	Master Jinpyo bestowed Buddhist precepts from Bodhisattva Ksitigarbha and Bodhisattva Maitreya 진표 율사, 지장·미륵보살로부터 수계
644	Master Uisang ordains as a Buddhist monk at Hwangbok-sa Temple 의상 대사 황복사에서 출가	751	Kim Daeseong begins construction of Bulguk-sa Temple and Seokgur-am Hermitage in Gyeongju 김대성, 경주 불국사·석굴암 건립 시작
645	Great Master Uisang and Master Wonhyo endeavored to study in Tang China 의상 대사, 원효 대사와 함께 당나라 유학 시도	774	Bulguk-sa Temple and Seokgur-am in Gyeongju near completion 경주 불국사·석굴암이 거의 완성됨
645	Establishment of Nine-Story Wooden Pagoda at Hwangnyong-sa by Queen Seondeok of Silla, as advised by Great Master Jajang 선덕여왕이 자장 율사의 건의로 황룡사 9층 목탑 건립	776	Restoration of Beopju-sa Temple by Master Jinpyo's disciples, including Ven. Yeongsim 진표 율사의 제자 영심 등이 법주사 중창
646	Establishment of Tongdo-sa Temple by Great Master Jajang 자장 율사, 통도사 창건	802	Establishment or restoration of Haein-sa Temple by Master Suneung 순응 스님의 해인사 창건(혹은 중창)
650	Master Uisang successfully completes his studies in Tang China after his second attempt. Prince Beopmin, who later became King Munmu, is dispatched as an envoy to Tang China 의상 대사, 두 번째 당나라 유학 시도 성공. 법민(후에 문무왕), 당에 사신으로 파견	875	Establishment of Seonam-sa Temple and Daeheung-sa Temple by Master Doseon (speculation) 도선의 선암사 및 대흥사 창건설
671	Master Uisang returns to Silla with the news of Tang China's intent to invade. Establishment of Naksan-sa Temple by Master Uisang after a personal audience with Avalokitesvara Bodhisattva	883	Enshrinement of two seated wooden Vairocana Buddha statues at Haein-sa Temple 해인사에서 두 구의 목조비로자나불좌상이 조성
		887	Choe Chiwon composes *Sangchanbyeongseo* of Bulguk-sa

Temple, the records of the enshrinement of the statues of Vairocana Buddha, Buddhistattva Manjusri, Buddhistattva Samantabhadra, and Amitabha Buddha
최치원, 불국사 「비로자나·문수·보현상찬병서」 및 「아미타불상찬병서」 지음

895 Establishment of *Myogilsangtap* Pagoda at Haein-sa Temple
해인사 묘길상탑 건립

897 Reconstruction of Haein-sa Temple
해인사 중건

936 Unification of the Later Three Kingdoms by King Taejo Wanggeon of Goryeo
왕건이 후삼국을 통일함

1024 Composition of *Record of Mugujeonggwangtap Pagoda Restoration* at Bulguk-sa Temple (excavated from *Seokgatap* or Sakyamuni Buddha Pagoda)
불국사 「무구정광탑중수기」 작성 (석가탑 출토)

1038 Composition of *Survey on the Restoration of Seoseoktap Pagoda* at Bulguk-sa Temple (excavated from *Seokgatap*, or Sakyamuni Buddha Pagoda)
불국사 「서석탑중수형지기」 작성 (석가탑 출토)

1085 Master Uicheon leaves to study in Song China
의천 스님, 송나라로 유학

1088 Reconstruction of Seonam-sa Temple by Master Uicheon
의천 스님이 선암사 중창

1170 Military coup occurs in Goryeo, which places King Myeongjong on the throne
무신정변 일어남

1172 Reconstruction of Magok-sa Temple by National Preceptor Jinul and his disciple Ven. Suu (speculation)
보조국사 지눌, 제자 수우와 마곡사 중창설

1232 Buin-sa Temple in Daegu, which enshrines the First Edition of Tripitaka Koreana, was burnt down by Mongolian invaders
몽골의 침입으로 초조대장경을 봉안했던 대구 부인사가 불에 탐

1235 The Chief Commander Kim Yisaeng and Sirang Yu Seok witness the *sarira* of Sakyamuni Buddha enshrined inside the pagoda at Diamond Ordination Platform at Tongdo-sa Temple
대장군 김이생, 시랑 유석이 통도사 금강계단의 진신사리를 확인

1237 Engraving of the Tripitaka Koreana (*Palman Daejanggyeong*) begins
팔만대장경 조성사업 시작

1238 Destruction of Hwangnyong-sa Temple by Mongolian invaders
몽골 침입으로 황룡사 소실

1326 Master Jigong of India pays homage to the *Geumgang gyedan* at Tongdo-sa Temple
인도의 지공 선사가 통도사 금강계단에 참배

1358 Partial destruction of Buseok-sa Temple by Japanese raiders
부석사, 왜구의 침입으로 일부 소실

1361 King Gongmin fled the royal palace to Andong. Restoration of the Buddhist altar in *Daeung-jeon* Hall at Bongjeong-sa Temple
공민왕, 안동으로 몽진. 봉정사 대웅전 불단 수리

1363 Relocation of the sacred *sarira* of Sakyamuni Buddha from Tongdo-sa Temple to Beopju-sa Temple by King Gongmin
Restoration of the *Geungnak-jeon* Hall roof at Bongjeong-sa Temple
공민왕이 통도사의 진신사리 1과를 법주사에 옮겨 봉안
봉정사 극락전 지붕 중수

1376	Restoration of *Muryangsu-jeon* Hall at Buseok-sa Temple 부석사 무량수전 중수
1377	Reconstruction of *Josa-dang* at Buseok-sa Temple 부석사 조사당 중건
1392	Establishment of Joseon 조선 건국
1398	Relocation of Tripitaka Koreana (*Palman Daejanggyeong*) from Ganghwa-do Island to Haein-sa Temple 팔만대장경판을 강화도에서 해인사로 옮김
1428	Illustration of the Descent of Maitreya Buddha (*Mireuk hasaengdo*) painted in *Daeung-jeon* Hall at Bongjeong-sa Temple 봉정사 대웅전 미륵하생도 조성
1458	King Sejo publishes 50 copies of Tripitaka Koreana at Haein-sa Temple 세조, 해인사 대장경 50부 간행
1464	King Sejo visits Bokcheon-am Hermitage at Beopju-sa Temple and Master Shinmi and his disciples Ven. Hakyeol and Ven. Hakjo hold a Great Dharma Assembly 세조가 법주사 복천암에 행차하자 신미대사가 제자 학열·학조 등과 대설법회를 개최
1490	Restoration of Josadang at Buseok-sa Temple Reconstruction of depositories completed for the Tripitaka Koreana Woodblocks (*Janggyeong Panjeon*) at Haein-sa Temple 부석사 조사당 중수 현재의 해인사 장경판전 중건 완료
1587	The first casting of the Bronze Bell in Daeheung-sa Temple. The bell was cast again in 1717 and 1772. 대흥사 동종 주조(1717년 및 1772년에 다시 주조함)
1588	Restoration of *Hwaeom gangdang* at Bongjeong-sa Temple 봉정사 화엄강당 중수

1593	The Japanese armies seize the sacred *sarira* of Sakyamuni Buddha enshrined in *Geumgang gyedan* at Tongdo-sa Temple during the invasion of Korea, Imjin War. 임진왜란 중 왜군이 통도사 금강계단 진신사리를 탈취
1604	Parinirvana of Master Seosan. The master implored that his robe and alms bowl be bequeathed to Daeheung-sa Temple Master Samyeong negotiates with Japan to return Korean prisoners of war and the sacred *sarira* of Sakyamuni Buddha 서산대사가 입적하며 의발을 대흥사에 전하라는 유지를 남김 사명대사가 일본으로 건너가 담판으로 포로 및 진신사리를 되찾아옴
1605	Restoration of *Palsang-jeon* and other pavilions at Beopju-sa Temple destroyed during the Japanese invasion was initiated by Master Samyeong and completed in 1626 임진왜란 당시 소실된 법주사 팔상전 등을 1626년까지 사명대사가 중창
1610	Parinirvana of Master Samyeong 사명대사 입적
1612	Construction of the stupa and stele of Master Samyeong at Hongje-am Hermitage in Haein-sa Temple. Inscription created by Heo Gyun 해인사 홍제암에 사명대사탑과 비 건립. 비문은 허균이 지음
1612	Construction of Wooden Seated Amitabha Buddha and Seated Bhaisajyaguru Buddha (Medicine Buddha) in *Daeung-jeon* Hall by the sculptor-monk Taejeon at Daeheung-sa Temple 조각승 태전, 대흥사 대웅전 목조아미타·약사여래좌상 조성
1624	Restoration of Beopju-sa Temple by Ven. Byeogam Gakseong Construction of the Seated Buddha Vairocana Triad Sculptures in *Daeungdaegwangbo-jeon* Hall, Beopju-

sa Temple by the Ven. Hyeonjin
벽암 각성에 의한 법주사 중창
조각승 현진, 법주사 대웅대광보전
소조삼불상 조성

1651 Reconstruction of Magok-sa Temple by Master Gaksun after being destroyed during the Japanese invasion
왜란으로 소실된 마곡사를 각순 스님이 중창

1655 Construction of Wooden Statue of Seated Avalokitesvara Bodhisattva in *Wontongbo-jeon* Hall at Beopju-sa Temple
법주사 원통보전 목조관음보살좌상 조성

1660 Reconstruction of Seonam-sa Temple halls, which were demolished during the Japanese invasion. Initiation of the project by Masters Gyeongjam, Gyeongjun, and Munjeong, and Master Chimgoeng later supervises the reconstruction project.
왜란으로 소실된 선암사 전각들이 경준·경잠·문정 스님에 의해 중건되고, 침굉 스님이 이어 받음

1667 Reconstruction of *Daeungbo-jeon* Hall at Daeheung-sa Temple by Master Simsu
심수 스님, 대흥사 대웅보전 중건

1686 The author of *Diary in the Mountains*, Jeong Sihan, visits Haein-sa Temple and leaves a record
『산중일기』의 저자 정시한이 해인사 방문하고 기록 남김

1687 Creation of Hanging Scroll Painting of Magok-sa Temple by six painter-monks, including Ven. Neunghak and Ven. Gyeho
능학·계호 등6인의 불화승에 의해 마곡사 석가모니괘불탱 조성

1695 Outbreak of a large fire at Haein-sa Temple
해인사에 큰 불이 남

1699 Establishment of a new hall at Seonam-sa Temple by Master Hoam, along with the enshrinement of various Buddha statues and paintings
호암 스님이 선암사에 새로운 전각을 짓고, 불상·불화를 다수 조성함

1700 Casting of the Bronze Bell at Seonam-sa Temple
선암사 동종 조성

1707 Monument installed to commemorate the restoration of Seonam-sa Temple
선암사 중수비 건립

1713 Completion of *Seungseon-gyo* Bridge by Master Hoam at Seonam-sa Temple
호암 스님이 선암사 승선교 완공

1719 *Ilju-mun* Gate installed at Seonam-sa Temple
선암사 일주문 건립

1729 Painting of the Vulture Peak Assembly (*Yeongsan hoesangdo*) created at Haein-sa Temple by the painter-monk Uigyeom
불화승 의겸, 해인사 영산회상도 조성

1736 Painting of *Gamrowangdo* (The King of Sweet Dew Painting) at Seonam-sa Temple created by painter-monk Ven. Uigyeom
불화승 의겸, 선암사 서부도암 감로도 조성

1740 Inscription of *Chronicles of Bulguk-sa* (*Bulguksa gogeum changgi*) by Master Dongeun
동은 스님, 『불국사고금창기』 저술

1743 Outbreak of large fire at Haein-sa Temple
해인사에 큰 불이 남

1753 Creation of Hanging Scroll Painting of Sakyamuni Buddha at Seonam-sa Temple
선암사 괘불탱 조성

1755 Lee Gwangsa sent away in exile for his involvement in the Writing on the Wall Case or Naju mural case (*Naju Gwaeseo Sageon*)
이광사, 나주벽서사건에 연루되어 유배됨

1782	Destruction of *Daegwangbo-jeon* Hall at Magok-sa Temple 마곡사 대광보전 소실
1789	Establishment of *Pyochungsa* at Daeheung-sa Temple in honor of Master Seosan; "*Pyochungsa*(表忠祠)" signboard was written and presented by King Jeongjo. 대흥사에 서산대사를 기리는 표충사를 건립하고 정조가 친필 편액을 하사함
1790	Birth of Prince Sunjo, son of King Jeongjo, after a 100-day prayer by Master Nulam at Seonam-sa Temple 선암사 눌암대사가 원통전에서 100일 기도를 드린 후 정조의 아들 순조 탄생
1813	Reconstruction of *Daegwangbo-jeon* Hall at Magok-sa Temple Reconstruction of *Cheonbul-jeon* Hall at Daeheung-sa Temple 마곡사 대광보전 재건 대흥사 천불전 중건
1818	Some statues of the Thousand Buddhas to be enshrined in *Cheonbul-jeon* Hall at Daeheung-sa Temple was blown off course to Japan on their way from Gyeongju, returning safely to Daeheung-sa Temple on a later date Reconstruction of *Daejeokgwang-jeon* Hall a year after the 1817 fire at Haein-sa Temple 대흥사 천불전에 모실 천불을 경주에서 옮겨오다 일부가 일본에 표류했으나 무사히 봉안함 해인사의 큰 불(1817년)이 나고, 이듬해 대적광전을 새로 지음
1823	Destruction of Seonam-sa Temple halls by a great fire Composition of the *History of Daedun-sa Temple*(Daedunsaji) by Jeong Yakyong, Master Choui, and others 선암사, 대화재로 대부분의 전각 소실 정약용, 초의선사 등이 『대둔사지』 집필

1824	Reconstruction of *Daeung-jeon* Hall and *Wontong-jeon* Hall at Seonam-sa Temple 선암사 대웅전, 원통전 등 중건
1840	Chusa Kim Jeonghui visits Daeheung-sa Temple on his way to exile 추사 김정희, 유배길에 대흥사 방문
1842	Restoration of *Yeongsan-jeon* Hall at Magok-sa Temple Restoration of Ilji-am Hermitage by Master Choui at Daeheung-sa Temple 마곡사 영산전 중수 초의선사, 대흥사 일지암 중수
1851	Composition of *Record of the Plan for Magok-sa Temple*(Magoksa Sajeokiban) 「마곡사사적입안」이 쓰여짐
1939	Construction of a colossal statue of Maitreya Buddha(Mireuk daebul) initiated by Kim Bokjin at Beopju-sa Temple 김복진, 법주사 미륵대불 조성 시작
2018	Listing of Buddhist Mountain Monasteries of Korea as a UNESCO World Heritage Site 한국의 산지승원, 유네스코 세계유산에 등재

SANSA

UNESCO WORLD HERITAGE
TEMPLES OF KOREA

© Association of Korean Buddhist Orders, 2021

First Edition	January 7, 2021
Produced by	Association of Korean Buddhist Orders
	3F, 45-19, Ujeongguk-ro, Jongno-gu, Seoul, Korea
	Tel. +82-2-732-4885, Fax. +82-2-737-7872
Published by	Bulkwang Publishing
	3F, 45-13, Ujeongguk-ro, Jongno-gu, Seoul, Korea
	Tel. +82-2-420-3300, Fax. +82-2-420-3400
Written by	Soowan Joo
Translated by	Heewon Park
Proofreading by	June Park, Sam Lacy, Jongbok Yi
Illusted by	Yongcheol Seo
Designed by	Koodamm

ISBN 979-89-7479-879-6 03220

US $42 ₩23,000